Delivering
the Sermon

Elements of Preaching

O. Wesley Allen Jr., series editor

Delivering
the Sermon

Voice, Body, and Animation in Proclamation

Teresa L. Fry Brown

Fortress Press
Minneapolis

DELIVERING THE SERMON
Voice, Body, and Animation in Proclamation

Cover image: © iStockphoto.com/Igor Skrynnikov
Cover and book design: John Goodman

Library of Congress Cataloging-in-Publication Data
Brown, Teresa L. Fry, 1951–
    Delivering the sermon : voice, body, and animation in proclamation / Teresa L. Fry Brown.
        p. cm. — (Elements of preaching)
    Includes bibliographical references.
    ISBN 978-0-8006-0447-9 (alk. paper)
    1. Preaching. I. Title.
    BV4211.3.B765 2008
    251'.03—dc22
                                        2008029740

The paper used in this publication meets the minimum requirements of American National Standard for Information Sciences—Permanence of Paper for Printed Library Materials, ANSI Z329.48-1984.

Manufactured in the U.S.A.

12   11   10   09   2   3   4   5   6   7   8   9   10

Contents

I Z Z 5 0 G

Editor's Foreword

Preparing beginning preachers to stand before the body of Christ and proclaim the word of God faithfully, authentically, and effectively Sunday after Sunday is and always has been a daunting responsibility. As North American pastors face pews filled with citizens of a postmodern, post-Christendom culture, this teaching task becomes even more complex. The theological, exegetical, and homiletical skills that preachers need for the future are as much in flux today as they have ever been in Western Christianity. Thus providing seminary students with a solid but flexible homiletical foundation at the start of their careers is a necessity.

Traditionally, professors of preaching choose a primary introductory textbook that presents a theology of proclamation and a process of sermon development and delivery from a single point of view. To maintain such a singular point of view is the sign of good writing, but it does at times cause problems for learning in pluralistic settings. One approach to preaching does not fit all. Yet a course simply surveying all of the homiletical possibilities available will not provide a foundation on which to build either.

Furthermore, while there are numerous introductory preaching textbooks from which to choose, most are written from the perspective of Euro-American males. Classes supplement this view with smaller homiletical texts written by women and persons of color. But a pedagogical hierarchy is nevertheless set up: the white male voice provides the main course and women and persons of color provide the side dishes.

Elements of Preaching is a series designed to help professors and students of preaching—including established preachers who want to develop their skills in specific areas—construct a sound homiletical foundation in a conversational manner. This conversation is meant to occur at two levels. First, the series as a whole deals with basic components found in most introductory preaching classes: theology of proclamation, homiletical contexts, biblical interpretation, sermonic claim, language and imagery, rhetorical form, delivery, and worship. But each element is presented by a different scholar, all of whom represent diversity in terms of gender, theological traditions (Baptist, Disciple of Christ, Lutheran, Presbyterian, and United Methodist), and ethnicity (African American, Asian American, and Euro-American). Instead of bringing in different voices at the margin of the preaching class, Elements of Preaching creates a conversation around the central topics of an introductory course without foregoing essential instruction concerning sermon construction and embodiment. Indeed, this level of conversation is extended beyond the printed volumes through the Web site www.ElementsofPreaching.com.

Second, the individual volumes are written in an open-ended manner. The individual author's particular views are offered but in a way that invites, indeed demands, the readers to move beyond them in developing their own approaches to the preaching task. The volumes offer theoretical and practical insights, but at the last page it is clear that more must be said. Professors and students have a solid place to begin, but there is flexibility within the class (and after the class in ministry) to move beyond these volumes by building on the insights and advice they offer.

In this volume, Teresa L. Fry Brown helps readers move from the study to the pulpit, from preparation to proclamation. Bringing together knowledge drawn from her work as a speech language pathologist, preacher, and professor of homiletics, she offers a melding of theology, communication theory, and speech techniques for preachers to improve the speaking and embodiment of their sermons. Preachers will benefit not only by engaging the descriptive and prescriptive discourse in *Delivering the Sermon*, they will be able to test their strengths and improve on weaknesses by using the practical exercises Fry Brown includes throughout the volume and on the Elements of Preaching Web site.

O. Wesley Allen Jr.

Introduction

My mouth fell open as I raised my head from scanning the sermon evaluation sheet just in time to see the five-foot-six, slender, alabaster, hairless, ordinarily quiet student removing his shirt as he began to describe Peter jumping overboard to attempt his famous walk on water. The students smiled, gasped, fell silent as Myron continued disrobing down to his shorts, his voice quaking and his face flushing to bright red. His intent was to symbolize the words of the text but his appearance and obvious embarrassment were a distraction that overshadowed the content of his sermon. He had used this preaching style several times in his home church and it was accepted as an appropriate means of transmitting the gospel. But here, Myron had neglected to assess the variety of people in the class, many of whom would find the format disturbing.

Veronica, a black female student, marched confidently to the pulpit. A Baptist preacher for ten years, she knew how to use her background as a public relations corporate executive to make immediate engagement with her listeners and work the room. Bringing the text to life with her passion, panning the entire room in an effort to connect with each person, punctuating the air with gestures, emphasizing emotion with her face and arms, immersing the listener in the depths of the text, and raising the sermon to a hopeful conclusion, this preacher had her listeners on the edges of their seats. She deftly used humor, volume adjustments, and image-rich language to deliver her exegetical insights. Her volume ebbed and flowed like an ocean tide. Each word was spoken with conviction. She invited each listener to journey with her through the text by her mere confident and engaging presence. The class seemed to hang on her every word, applauding as she finished the sermon. She was able to deliver a dynamic sermon to a receptive audience—a different experience for a preacher who rarely had an opportunity to preach in her home church.

The class responded with barely audible "Amen," "It's alright," "Take your time," and "You can do it," as Frank struggled to begin his sermon. He had had panic attacks before but this time he resolved to preach his sermon in spite of his nervousness. Small tremors began to grip the edges of his mouth but he kept going. The spasms increased to engulf his entire body, undulating upward from his knees to his eyelids. He struggled for air, and at first I thought he was having a full-fledged seizure, but he kept going. His breathing was labored as he launched into the body of the sermon. He broke out in a sweat, occasionally hiccoughed, and I thought the paramedic call was not far behind. He stood still, gripping the podium as he completed his twelve-minute oral presentation, then he quickly sat down and hung his head. He had sought medical help and was told that it was a psychological issue. He was in therapy and was trying to overcome his fear of public speaking. He explained that for the five years of his preaching ministry every sermon was like this major presentation. He pastored a small Baptist church in Birmingham, Alabama, where his congregation was supportive of his preaching and had become accustomed to his tremors. His call to preach superseded his obvious delivery issues. The peer evaluations were amazing. They were not put off by his physicality and were able to understand the sermon. His resolve to preach in spite of his idiosyncrasies increased their desire to listen.

The typical twenty-first-century "Introduction to Preaching" class is vastly diverse in student ethnicity, age, gender, denomination, theology, role models, and preaching experience—a diversity increasingly reflected in our church pulpits. Sermon delivery style is no longer a matter of "one size fits all." The role of the preacher is to assist the listeners in the identification of spiritual, social, cultural, psychological, and economic issues that have an impact on daily life. There are as many different styles of delivery as students present in the class or preachers in the pulpit. Delivering the sermon entails basic knowledge of communication and the preacher's use of voice and diction to transmit the message. In the midst of singular definitions of "good" preaching, the study of communication is an essential tool for sound delivery of the good news. The content of the sermon may be excellent, the context fully understood, the exegesis may lead biblical scholars to cheer, but a weak delivery can overshadow all the preliminaries.

My profession as a teacher and practitioner in speech-language pathology has given me expertise in phonation and sound production, human transmission systems, sound perception or hearing, and acoustic, physiological, psychological, and linguistic phenomena of human speech. Part of the profession is proficiency in the measurement and assessment of intelligibility and quality, technological processing of speech analysis, synthesis, and automatic recognition and therapeutic principles for remediation of communicative disorders in children and adults. It was not until 1986 that my profession as a speech pathologist and my profession of faith would intersect, when a homiletics professor asked me to assess his class for possible voice and diction difficulties and recommend ways in which they could improve in their communication of sermonic material or sacred rhetoric. Rhetoric as classically defined is the art or study of using language effectively and persuasively. Sermons are basically an arrangement of sounds, words, movements, and even silence used to communicate faith claims. The preacher's ability to transmit these faith claims or beliefs clearly and effectively assists the listener in processing the message. This is one reason the specialized use of the vocal mechanism in speaking and singing must be afforded particular attention in sermon delivery. Cicero writes that persuasive speech is marked by invention, arrangement, style, memory, and delivery of language.[1] One's ability to communicate a message clearly and effectively is directly affected by the type of voice and diction one possesses. Oral competence is grounded in the intentions of the speaker and receptivity of the listener as he seeks to know what the preacher thinks or feels. In other words, when the preacher's delivery is marked by obscure meaning, monotone delivery, misarticulation of sound, mispronunciation of words in the biblical text, insufficient volume, or failure to consider the language levels or abilities of the listener, the sermon—regardless of the proficiency of exegesis, depth of poetic creativity, or brilliance of attire—will suffer disruptions in communication.

The communication process of preaching begins as the preacher cognitively processes what he or she is going to say, whether through an assigned text or personal choice of Scripture or theme. Parts of speech are then placed in a learned or socially acceptable order. Language is chosen to relate these thoughts based on ethnicity, race, gender, education, age, and ability of one's listeners. Information is prepared to be transmitted to those who share the same coding system and seek the message. The prepared sermon content then may be either accepted or rejected by the listener.

The voice of the preacher must be appropriate to the age, gender, and physicality of the listener or the communication channel is disrupted. That is, the speaker's intelligibility of sounds, omission of sounds or syllables, distortion of phonemes, additional consonants or vowels due to regional, racial, or cultural dialects, language development, or educational level have an impact on communication channels. Moreover, the level and range of the preacher's speaking voice, appropriate loudness, the distinctive quality of the preacher's voice in terms of smoothness, pacing, energy, inflection, emotion, or tonality, "culturally accepted" vocabulary, slang, idioms, acronyms or syntax in particular contexts determine the efficiency of the vocalizations.[2]

The contemporary landscape is filled with conflicting images and proclamation intent. That is, the intent of the gospel is for *all* persons. For example, chronic use of "men" without regard for the presence of "women" in the sermon delivery excludes a significant portion of humanity in reception of the "good news." Moreover, the styles, mannerisms, attire, and even gender demographics of both preachers and parishioners have changed over the past twenty years. Preachers are in search of their distinctive, unique, particular voice for this day and age. This book introduces preachers to the rationale and methods for effective use of voice (verbal) and body (nonverbal) in the animation of the word in the preaching moment. Each chapter opens with typical examples from preaching courses (like the one used above) to help frame the issues to be discussed.

Chapter 1, "Communicating the Word," reviews basic communication theory, speech development, and oral-aural language. It also discusses the importance of figures of speech, verbal communication, inclusive language, and the power of language in the preached word. The basis of the discussion will be questions beginning preachers frequently ask regarding the whys and hows of communication in the preaching moment.

Chapter 2, "Inculturating the Word," covers cultural variables involving preachers and congregational contexts. These variables include gender, race, ethnicity, geography, denomination, congregational composition, age, education, and electronic (Internet and television) communication.

Chapter 3, "Voicing the Word," includes respiration, hearing, vocal energy, breath control, pitch, volume, pacing, rate, pausing, intensity, duration, rhythm, intonation, and inflection. Special attention is given to identifying one's own voice.

Chapter 4, "Articulating the Word," presents information on basic articulation, phonation, mood, flavor, color, quality, tone, clarity, dialect, and vernacular. It also addresses commonly mispronounced words in preaching and lists suggestions for increased clarity of speech.

Chapter 5, "Embodying the Word," discusses emotion and preaching, mood, facial expression, eye contact, posture, amplification, anxiety, text, sermon, and manuscript form and usage. Brief mention will be made of the connection between sermon form and worship style (liturgical to extemporaneous).

Chapter 6, "Animating the Word," will contain information about physicality (attire, body type, hair, and clothing), kinesics (body movement, gestures, self-touching, and posture), chronemics (meaning, structure and use of time, speed of body movement), haptics (tactile, interpersonal physical contact with listeners, touch), and proxemics (space, distance between preacher and listener).

Suggestions and exercises for enhancing voice, diction, and nonverbal engagement of the listener are included in each chapter. I have used these exercises in preaching seminars and classes I have taught over the course of the last twenty years and these may be used for group discussions or for individual enhancement of sermon delivery. They may be modified to fit the context and interest of the readers.

Chapter 1

Communicating the Word

Jefferson is a black male who grew up in a Baptist church in Ohio. His primary preaching models are older black males who evidence a slow, hoarse, staccato, yet rhythmic cadence in preaching. He is caught between his "proper" academic speech and his acculturated speech pattern. The result is an odd blend of "standard" English pronunciation of some words on the one hand, and a regional-cultural dialect—omission of word endings, substitution of /f/ for /th/—on the other hand. Part of the class verbally responds positively to his rhetorical style, but part of the class seems to have lost something in the cultural translation.

Elizabeth stands stock still, barely raising her head as she begins to read the text in a barely audible monotone. She is a diminutive white female preaching her first time in public. She apologizes for what she is about to say and repeatedly pleas for forgiveness as she gives her views on the text. Her articulation is flawless, but her energy level borders on flatlining. After ten minutes of wandering through the text she abruptly stops and takes her seat. She clearly communicated her fear, but any sermonic intent was lost.

Terry eagerly approaches the front of the classroom, lays his sermon manuscript on the podium, and proceeds to preach while walking back and forth across the front of the room. He leans on the podium once or twice as he points toward the listener or uses both hands to form a concept. He seems to have memorized his text and looks at each classmate as he clearly and concisely relates the good news. His facial expressions and gestures mirror the emotions in the text. He pauses for effect and paces his words as if he is sharing the best news he has ever heard.

Language 101

Language is the study of sound production in nature and the means by which it is perceived, received, analyzed, processed, and responded to by another entity. In human communication this transmission of information may occur through hearing, body movements, eye contact, technological media, touch, cultural rules, experience with the information sender, or other channels. The efficacy of language is dependent on the quality, quantity, and timing of such information transmission.

Language is a means of self-expression and disclosure and falls into two main categories: receptive language (understanding what is said, written, or signed) and expressive language (speaking, writing, or signing). *Orality* is spoken language. *Aurality* is word connection with the listener. One chooses and uses words, pictures, signs, objects, emotions, and beliefs that the listener or receiver understands and then chooses to ignore or to respond to the intent of the communication. Words are present, dynamic, living verbal and nonverbal signs, signals, and symbols that represent the climate of beliefs, attitudes, values, common sense, common talk. Verbal communication is direct, immediate, and interdependent feedback or understanding of the message.

Language provides a means for building community between speakers and listeners.[1] Linguist Ludwig Wittgenstein calls the communicative act a "language game" with a set of moves, rules of usage, and possibilities for changing the rules of engagement.[2] The language interaction is a space for transmission of thoughts. This chapter will review the basics of communication theory, speech development, and oral-aural language. It will also discuss the importance of verbal and nonverbal communication as part of the preached word. The discussion grows out of questions students and preaching seminar participants frequently ask regarding the *whys* and *hows* of communication in the preaching moment.

Preaching Communication 101

In basic communication theory there is a sender (preacher/proclaimer/speaker) and a receiver (congregant/listener). Sacred rhetoric is transmitted through various oral and written communication channels or conveyances: sermons, scholarly commentaries, multimedia recordings, plays, denominational position papers, small-group discussions, Bible studies, art, music, and various translations of the biblical text. Preaching is an oral medium for sharing faith-centered messages. Preaching is informational and dialogical, melding the call and response of preacher and congregant. In order for this paradigm to work properly, however, there must be a sense of mutuality (see fig. 1.1).

Both parties send and receive information in a feedback loop or two-way communicative flow.

Figure 1.1 • Basic Communication Paradigm

The sender initiates the communication, understanding that the receiver is ready to listen. The congregant trusts the preacher to impart information without force, manipulation, prejudice, or offense. The speaker awaits feedback from the receiver. The receiver may use *nonverbal cues*, such as a nod, turning the body, facial expression, physical gesture, or *verbal cues*, such as saying *Amen* or some other sort of vocalized assent, to let the speaker know that message was received, affirmed, and/or understood.[3] This feedback loop, or call and response, continues as the conversation either builds or terminates.

The form, intensity, and duration of the exchange of information are based on the relationship and experience of the speaker and the listener. Language is relational. Because language is socially shaped through traditional and/or contemporary values and usage, it allows people to experience their concept of reality,[4] shapes human consciousness, and organizes a person's world. Language has the power to bring about changes in perspectives or worldview.

Religious language is a distinct type of relational discourse that theologian Paul Van Buren describes as "a fruitful source of rule breaking." It is a means of attempting to describe God and faith issues in imperfect yet creative ways. The speaker bends the language to express a sense of reality that exists beyond what can be seen, felt, or even fully understood. She walks the edge of meaning to talk insightfully about spiritual realities and understands that word-meaning changes with the setting, context, or community.[5] Religious language is consciously retrospective as persons strive to relate clearly their beliefs. It is demonstrative in its orthodoxy and identity as exemplified in prayers, invocations, sermons, and songs. It is imaginative and exploratory as the speaker responds to existential claims of belief.[6] However, religious language may also be filled with sound and fury signifying nothing when the verbosity of the speaker overshadows the intent of the message. It may be groundbreaking as new words are created in the delivery of homiletical material or monotonous due to obscure, inert, elitist, or canned linguistic rudiments.

Individual preachers use language in different ways and exhibit different points of communicability. They utilize language based on their experience, comfort level, role models, and physical ability. In *Orality and Literacy: The*

Technologizing of the Word, linguist Walter Ong states that language allows humans to voice experiences in concrete terms, to enflesh experience in sensory imagery.[7]

Each of the preachers described above attempted to express his or her theology and textual understanding, and to address a faith issue in the context of a classroom of diverse listeners. It is important to understand that what works in one situation will fail miserably in another if one is unaware of the dynamics of language.

Language in the Preaching Moment

In the "language game" of preaching, the preacher and congregation exchange faith talk in a give and take, call and response, verbal and nonverbal, vocal and nonvocal, and logical and emotive manner. The preacher must *mine the deep.* He or she should spend time listening to the language pattern of the congregation and considering ascribed and actual patterns of faith talk: What is the primary translation of the biblical text used in the worship services? Is the language formal or informal? Is the language of faith exclusive to select groups or inclusive of all persons? What names for God hold primacy? Who holds the power to engage in or end the conversation, the preacher or the listeners? Who speaks most often in a worship experience? Are there portions of the liturgy reserved only for ordained persons? If so, whom and why? The words of the preacher must be in the language of the people, the vernacular. This facilitates a participatory, inviting interchange between the preacher as oral interpreter of the written text and the people as cultural interpreters of the message. In the preaching moment numerous elements of language—orality, aurality, semiotics (symbols and signs), and nonverbal language or meta-language—are interconnected, combined in a communicative channel with or without distractions and interference.

Preaching is communication in the concrete, filled with language and images from day-to-day details—dynamics, sights, sounds, smells, tastes, texture, and life-scenes. Preaching revisits the familiar through recognition of the frame of reference of listener and identity with the hearer's environment. One delivers the sermon in a manner in which the hearer is able to see and hear him- or herself within the sermon.[8] According to Henry Mitchell, preaching is "depth to depth" communication. Fred Craddock stipulates that preaching involves the self in "the longest trip a person takes is from head to heart."[9] Holistically, preaching involves issues of life that stir memories and plant new ideas in the hearer. For the pastor, preaching must involve an intimate, personal identification with the existential situation of the listeners, even to the point of gut-level emoting. Also, the preaching moment brings us face to face with

God. The efficacy of the sermon may lead to a reinforcement, correction, or transformation of the convictions the listeners already have as the speaker and the listener are invited to think again about beliefs. Using vivid, attractive, and engaging language enjoins the intellect and emotion as persons reconsider their faith.[10]

Language is manifest in rhetoric through a communication channel, encoding-decoding symbols, and signs between a speaker and listener. Joseph Webb, in *Preaching and the Challenge of Pluralism*, discusses "symbolicity," the signs and symbols of communication. *Signs*, he says, are sensory inputs that prompt our senses to respond. A red hexagon with white lettering is a stop sign. In the Bible, a miracle was thought to be a sign of a divine action. The star in the east was a sign of where the infant Jesus was born. *Symbols* represent something that is absent. The cross is a symbol of Jesus' sacrifice. Signs and symbols form the basis for human response to cultural, conscious, and visual stimuli. Each symbol stands for ethical, moral, religious, or cultural meaning.[11] Response to symbols is either positive or negative, cognitive, and emotive. In the preaching moment, "symbolicity" affects language production and nonverbal presentation.

The concept of *signification* assigns symbols to "mean" a thing or an idea. The signifier may speak in agreement with a point of view, while the tone of the voice creates doubt in the very act and word of agreement. For example, if the preacher is talking about the "joy of the Lord," a smile or facial expression that depicts exhilaration assists in communicating the emotion. The signifier adds comments to move the conversation in a particular direction, makes a comment that has nothing to do with the context of the discourse, or critiques or analyzes a particular person or group. Language signification or symbolization verbalizes a visual sign with many meanings, such as bread and wine as Christ's body and blood, or air meaning the Holy Spirit, or water as indicative of chaos or nurture. Language is *denotative*, effecting enhancing understanding of clarity, cultural imperatives, or common words. Language is *connotative*, through use of metaphor, images, symbols, dialogue, or ambiguity to "hook" the information being transmitted.[12]

Effective communication[13] in the preaching moment is grounded in cohesion. Both sides of the transmission know the forms and conventions of language. The communication has an intentionality of purpose. There is a valid reason for the sermon. It makes sense. The listener responds to what is said either through immediate verbal or vocal means or in a delayed manner through change in behavior or through increased learning. Both the preacher and listener are able to relate the information to other bodies of knowledge. A sermon is not preached in a vacuum. It is a living speech act and in some manner the information has been related before the present situation. The sermon undergirds the continuity of one's faith journey within a particular context.

Efficient Message Transmission

Basic communication theory speaks of a channel or media corridor for transmission of a message from one source to another. In preaching, God and the (hopefully) God-inspired message are central to a feedback loop between the preacher and congregation. Several factors impinge on whether or not the message is successfully communicated. The preacher should be aware of the multiple cultures and human elements present in any group of listeners. What is the age distribution of the listeners? How much older or younger than the average congregant is the preacher? Do the preacher and the listeners share values? In an age of transdenominationalism, what are the understood and actual denominational or belief affiliations of the listeners? In the twenty-first century, a significant portion of the faith community has shifted to denominations that possess a more syncretistic view of faith than was common in the early to mid-twentieth century. Similarities in gender, race, and sexuality between the congregation and preacher also enhance the preaching moment rather than diminish potential barriers between them. The reputation, personal status, education, experience, and familiarity of the preacher as perceived by the congregation at times provide an immediate rapport between the communicative parties, particularly when the majority of the congregation identifies with the preacher.

Finally, the message itself potentially enhances the communicative execution. The familiarity the preacher and congregation has with the text, the illustrative information, and the liturgical season each have an impact on the content of the message. How the preacher chooses language to denote humor, the length and genre of the sermon, the use of multimedia, manuscript or extemporaneous presentation may generate attentiveness to the sermon. The following diagram (fig. 1.2) illustrates the sermonic feedback loop.

Communication Disruptions

The factors listed in figure 1.2 are representative rather than exhaustive. There are a number of other factors that may have an impact on the transmission loop and either enhance or destroy the clarity of the message. Consider the way something as simple as the choice of the biblical text upon which the sermon is based can disrupt communication. Choice of a text may be predetermined by the local congregation, the liturgical season, the denomination, or the use of a particular lectionary, or the preacher may choose the text herself.

Figure 1.2 • Sermonic Feedback Loop

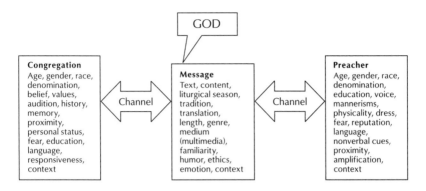

But one must remember that the contemporary church contains people with varying degrees of knowledge of the text. For example, at different ends of the spectrum are those who have no previous connection to the text and those who know the text well but have a distorted understanding of what the "text really says" and a different theology from the preacher. Both circumstances may result in resistance to the message. Also, the translation of the text read in worship can cause a disruption. If the preacher uses a paraphrase version in a congregation that traditionally uses the King James Version or the King James Version in a congregation used to contemporary critical translations, the listeners may feel a disconnect before the preacher even begins to speak her sermon.

Surface barriers to meaning are language, images, and appearance. Deeper barriers to meaning are anxieties, resistance, and defensiveness on the part of either the preacher or the listener. Static in the communication channel may emanate from the language meanings or type of language used in the tradition, by the preacher, or in the other elements of worship. Preachers have little power to control some of these, while they are responsible for others. Some examples that the preacher can influence include:

- Power and authority disparities between the preacher and the congregation
- Preconceived notions about the preacher's oratorical skill, reputation, personhood, or faith
- Condescending terminology, mood, tone, and presence in the sermon

- Noise emitted from the environment—something as minor as the hum of a heater or as disconcerting as a screeching, tinny microphone
- Sermonic humor (or what passes for humor), inappropriate or risqué language
- Varying theological worldviews and ethical stances between the preacher and congregation or among factions of the congregation
- Sermons that stop earlier or last longer than what the congregation generally expects and experiences
- Challenges from the preacher for a quiet congregation to respond or less verbal responses from the preacher in the midst of a vocally engaged congregation

In addition to these types of disruptions, there are a number of language signals of which the preacher must be aware and must address to enhance the effectiveness of the communication loop. Every preacher experiences one of these at some point, so understanding their possibility rather than striving for perfection is our goal.

- Incomplete sentences and inaccurate sentence structure (some simply lose the sentence on the page or in their head due to anxiety or some physical disruption)
- Incorrect pronouns, plurals, and possessives (at times this is a function of dialect or regionalism rather than incorrect speech)
- Omission of parts of a story or punchline (if it is your story you should know it well enough to retell it with or without hyperbole)
- Run-on sentences. (I usually caution students to edit down sentences. The longest one I counted in class was fifty-two words long. This affects the preacher's breathing cycle, sentence phrasing, and general reception of the majority of the sermon content, and often leaves the listener confused.)

The overall use of verbal and nonverbal language is vitally important to the transmission of the message. There are several basic guidelines for linguistically efficient sermons. In reviewing my notes from the only preaching class I took in seminary, I recall that Dr. Charles G. Adams, Senior Pastor of Hartford Memorial Baptist Church in Detroit, Michigan, in his authoritative voice, advised neophyte preachers on communicative sound in preaching. As I remember, he intoned:

- Don't be dull, tedious, or laborious
- Don't apologize for the sermon
- Don't be inaudible—reach the furthest person from the pulpit
- Don't preach at, under, or over the people, but to, with, and for the people
- Don't imitate others—be yourself
- Don't preach too long[14]

I have found these principles invaluable in the development of my preaching voice, and in maintaining relevant content and purposeful connection with the listeners. Each element takes into account both the needs of the listener and the authenticity of the preacher. The following exercise provides another way to consider all the players in the preaching communication paradigm.

⊛ Exercises for Communicating the Word

"Just" Text Selection and Use Exercise

In this exercise, select a pericope. Then reflect on the following questions:

- Read it in several translations out loud.
- How does the text parallel my context?
- What personal bias do I bring to this text?
- Does this text in any way slight or degrade any culture, gender, ethnic, national, denominational, social, economic, or age group?
- Will I be able to earnestly use this pericope and my imagery to help listeners view all persons as equals?
- Am I able to reframe the text in light of language that may "other" some listeners?

Foundations of the Preaching Moment Exercise

In sermon preparation, preachers do well to engage in self-interpretation and interpretation of their context before they turn to exegesis of the biblical text. A fuller list of the arenas of critical exegesis includes:

- exegesis of self
- exegesis of congregation
- exegesis of community
- exegesis of world
- exegesis of text
- exegesis of reception of the Word

Each of these stages should begin and end with prayer. After jotting notes about each area, prepare a sermon outline in consideration of the answers. Preachers need to engage in exercises in portability of communication—learning to tailor sermons for congregations that are both identical to and distinct from one another, especially congregations whose demographics are different from the context of one's "home" congregation.

Preaching is an opportunity to use God's gift of language to its fullest. Words affect the heart, soul, and mind. The preacher must be committed to oral communication, keeping words simple, clear, and appropriate. One must invite the listeners, both as individuals and as a community, into self-examination and fuller personal engagement of the biblical text. The preacher must relay hope for change from present realities to future possibilities. Finally, the preacher must lead the community in celebration of what God has done, is doing, and will do in their lives. The preacher seeks to open up means for all of God's children to stand on equal footing, which by necessity involve the critique of inequities in interpersonal relationships, families, communities, churches, and in the world.

Language is verbal and nonverbal signs, signals, symbols that represent the climate of beliefs, attitudes, values, common sense, common talk. It allows us to assign meaning to life. It makes creating order to our reality possible. The language of preaching must be carefully considered in order to support, inform, change, or broaden the listener's faith experience.

Chapter 2

Inculturating the Word

Sally, an international student, is soft-spoken, barely audible, and makes minimal eye contact. She is a former youth pastor from South Korea with five years experience, at times preaching three times on a Sunday. She folds her hands in a prayerful posture throughout the sermon. Her overall presentation is marked by spiritual depth, high regard for the preaching moment, excellent exegesis, and recurring narrative content bordering on a string of stories interwoven with the biblical text. Substitution errors such as /l/ for /r/ and general translation errors in word choice are also present.

Anandi is from Sri Lanka. He takes the preaching task seriously, almost reverently. He fully embodies the text for his sermon, including wearing traditional cultural attire even down to sandals. After discarding those sandals, he preaches about "beautiful feet" bringing good news. He slowly details the importance of ministry with precise British English articulation. His voice ranges from a quite whisper to an emotionally laden falsetto as he rises on his toes to talk about heralding God's word. The class fascination with his "exotic" appearance is lessened as he brings the text to life.

Shirley has significant experience as a preacher. She is an evangelist with a nondenominational, eponymous television ministry that appears on local cable access. Her theology is conservative, 1960s hellfire and brimstone—everyone who is not like her is going to hell. Shirley's language is exclusive: "man" for human beings, "He" for God, "Praise the Lord, saints," "impartation of the Spirit," "Jeezu" for Jesus—condemning language. She over-articulates each syllable ("mad-duh" for made) and appears to be playing to the camera every time she preaches, even when a camera is not present.

Each of these preachers represents a different aspect of twenty-first-century preaching culture. There is a veritable smorgasbord of preachers with varying cultures, styles, competencies, personas, and performative and linguistic abilities. Some, such as students from South Korea or various Asian or African countries, enter the preaching moment with an understanding of preaching that is vastly different from their U.S. counterparts. Their bicultural and bilingual engagement with English and American religious culture may contribute to theological and communication barriers during the preaching moment. Hearers may misinterpret the intentions and beliefs of preachers from other theological perspectives, visibly refusing to listen to some.

The number of students who appreciate or participate in televangelism also add to a broadened culture of sermon form and function. Some technological enhancements and presentations characterized by sound bites, intense, vivid imagery, or short-attention-span gimmicks are attractive to some and rejected by others who view preaching as sacred rather than secular rhetoric. Those from small rural churches or from churches with fewer than 250 members who effectively and faithfully preach without microphones, cameras, and soundboards may fill up a room with sound and short stories. Those from megachurches may be lost without a headset and large space for preaching. Their style and personality may be more effective on the Internet or in hologram.

The focus of this chapter is on variables that are evident in contemporary diverse cultures. These variables include gender, race, ethnicity, geography, denomination, congregational composition, age, and education. These variables translate into significant cultural variants in sermon content and delivery as well as in televangelism and other electronic (Internet and television) communication.

Defining Culture

My understanding of the concept of culture is that it is the foundation of our individual and collective existence. Culture is deeper than such social designations as name, address, social security number, zip code, area code, credit rating, social standing, marital status, alma mater, or occupation. Culture is the totality of who we are as individuals and collectives.[1] Culture is our genetic make-up, parentage, family configurations, and racial solidarity. Culture is the environment that we choose to live within, avoid living within, hold residence within by coincidence, or are barred from living within. Culture enables us to establish predictable and acceptable patterns of interaction. It is the basis for our ethical behavior and values systems. It is fundamental to who we are and reinforces our unique personhood. It distinguishes our actions in the world through our understanding of our history, the pantheon of our heroic members, our symbols of faith or belief, and the rituals that demonstrate that belief. Culture is our worldview, our way of making sense of our immediate and remote surroundings. People in varied cultures may hold differing views of destiny, freedom, agency, responsibility, honor, and dignity. And, especially important for our focus on preaching, culture is shaped by those with whom we verbally or nonverbally interact.

Anthropologist Clifford Geertz, in *The Interpretation of Cultures*, defines culture as "an historically transmitted pattern of meanings embodied in symbols, a system of inherited conceptions expressed in symbolic form by means of which humans communicate, perpetuate, and develop their knowledge about and attitudes towards life."[2] Culture is learned by experience, imitation, formal and informal instruction from parents, peers, media, authority figures, and self-selection. It distinguishes us from others based on contrasting values, age, gender, race, denomination, community, physical ability, sexuality, and ethnicity. Culture involves the training and refinement of one's mind, emotions, thoughts, and mannerisms by such social institutions as school, church, or other affiliated groups or institutions. Culture includes the concepts, habits, skills, art, instruments, institutions, and so forth of a given people in a given period.

Cross-cultural Preaching

Linguist Dell Hymes suggests that cultures possess communicative competencies for information sharing. The sender and receiver share rules of language structure, form, topic, and event within a given culture.[3] Communication is enhanced when both the speaker and listener understand the rules of engagement. Regardless of the land of origin of those communicating, basic communication is affected by factors such as gender, race, ethnicity, age, denomination, and so forth. Each person has a different perception of the world. There are those who never venture outside their community, church, family, or school. Some speak only their native tongue and have no intention of learning another language. These factors may limit their ability to communicate with those outside their culture or cultures.

Persons shaped by different cultures cognitively process information differently but may arrive at the same conclusion. The sermon flow may be difficult for some to follow, but in the end all may understand the intent of the message. On the other side of the coin, the particular ways in which preachers express ideas may impede the message. Some utilize present tense only while others relate events only in past tense. One generation may relate information in a formal, stylized, academic style while another uses informal, conversational style.

In today's world, *all* preaching is cross-cultural. The preacher therefore must have an awareness of the cultural subsystems present in the congregation. Differences are present even if all those present "look" or "sound" alike. The oral-aural traditions, vernacular, ethnocentrism, and cross-cultural language usage are established through listeners and speakers, dialect, regionalisms, "in-language,"[4] age, gender, geography, culture, race, class, education, comfort/preparation, and multiple language levels. Moreover, given the number of persons who neither hear nor speak in contemporary churches, the preacher must also be aware of how body language, or the lack thereof, transmits information. As Fred Craddock states, the listener completes the sermon.[5]

The ways in which one preacher may speak with authority and another may be "seeking permission" is determined by his or her communicative competency:

- The means of channeling the message (one preacher may demonstratively exhibit hesitancy and fear in the preaching moment, while another may boldly stand and effortlessly deliver the message)
- The context of the message (one might be more comfortable delivering a sermon in one's local church than in a seminary classroom)
- Who is sending (some listeners respond better to a familiar voice than a new or guest preacher)
- Who is receiving (the listener has his or her own levels of attentiveness and responsiveness that may not be in sync with the verbal style or rate of the preacher)
- The message's organization (there are sermons that follow very logical outlines while others are a random collection of thoughts)
- Content (the preacher must be aware not only of the topics and illustrations that connect with the listeners but also those some might find uncomfortable or offensive)
- Style (different audiences responds better to different delivery styles; a good preacher has a variety of styles in his or her homiletical repertoire)
- Various other cultural considerations (listener acceptance or rejection of sermons often has more to do with the differences in ethnic, gender, or racial characteristics of the preacher and congregation or preconceived notions about who can preach than the sermon content)

In short, bridging communicative gaps is as important to the preaching moment as exegesis of the text.

Cultural Language Considerations

In the African American preaching culture, there is a decided love for the beauty of language.[6] In this predominately oral culture, words are created and recreated like preparing a meal. The preacher seeks sounds and words that the people can hear and see. The ebb and flow of sermon delivery is built on the preacher's particular expressive mode, timing, pitch, pause, reflection, and pace. Depending on the audience, the preacher may be transparent in her preaching, expressing emotion, belief, and knowledge. Occasionally in multiethnic or denominational settings, the preacher masks her faith as a protective device against embarrassment, theological critique, or fear of being misunderstood.[7] The context of the sermon dictates the freedom of expression in the preacher.

Another cultural difference is the dialogical call and response inherent in black preaching. The preaching moment is not a solitary, performative act with the herald on a great stage as if he were Hamlet presenting a soliloquy, waiting for the end of the act and a rousing applause. In a communicative cycle one speaks and another listens and responds. The original speaker then counters the original listener's rejoinder and the pattern is established. The timing, rate, and volume of the exchange depend on both the speaker and the listener. In black preaching this cyclical pattern may be momentary, permeate the entire sermon, evolve as celebration increases, occur only at the end of a sermon, or be verbally absent. It is important to remember that call and response in the black church setting may be verbal, nonverbal, or both. People may wave a hand, clap, stand up, run, cry, shake their heads, rock back and forth, moan, hum, kneel, or even throw items at the preacher, in an affirming sort of way.

Musicologist Jon Michael Spencer details the folk mannerisms of black preaching. He says that the preacher begins in a normal speaking voice then modulates as momentum grows. He calls black preaching a "danced religion."[8] Call and response is not a planned activity, although there are some preachers who practice it and write sayings into their manuscripts. Call and response is like hearing a song—memories begin to flood your soul and before you know it, you are either humming the tune or attempting a dance you haven't done in ages. Call and response is evident outside of black culture. It is nonvocal in some predominately white congregations as people sit forward with their heads resting on their fists, smiling knowingly, softly laughing, and uttering barely audible "Amens." In more charismatic white churches, the pattern of call and response mirrors that of black churches with full body movements and vocal utterances in dialogue with the preached word. The dialogue is a verbally prompted mode of call and response evident in cross-cultural settings. The preacher instructs the listeners in bodily engagement ("Turn to your neighbor and say _____" or "Give somebody a high five") or vocalized assent to what has been preached ("Say, Amen") or read ("Repeat after me, '_____'"). One popular white female televangelist constantly peppers the sermon with "Look at someone and hit them upside the head." (I still cannot figure out why violence is perpetrated when one is preaching about the love of God. This is a prime example of a cultural difference.)

Gender and sexuality are other crucial cultural considerations. Gender questions concerning preaching abound. Do/should women preach differently than men? Do women sound like preachers? Is the content of women's sermons different from that of men? Is there a hidden agenda in sermons by gay and lesbians? Do we have to hear that justice stuff again? Is he a real preacher? Is there a place for a preacher with a soft voice or petite physique? In response to these sorts of questions, I ask for everyone to bring in a recording of God's voice, and we will take a vote on which one is right. The communication paradigm is hampered by listeners who dismiss the voices of women or sexual minority preachers as "ungodly."

The preacher's education, occupational background, and experience dictate the language level of the sermon. They also influence one's comfort with public speaking or group engagement. Men have more male preaching role models than women have female preaching role models. Some women respond by emulating masculine stance, voice production, pacing, dress, and mannerisms. Other women exhibit more controlled body language, dress in a feminine manner, and are less likely to use hard vocal contacts and loudness during the preaching moment. Women may be afforded less opportunity to preach if they do not imitate male models. Their sense of call may be muted by the authority figures. Those preachers with supportive family systems and denominational mentors preach with more confidence (not necessarily better) than those who are fighting to have their voices heard. The congregation, even when composed of a majority of women, may reject a preacher based on gender or sexuality due to preconceived notions of God and ordained ministry or theological biases regarding sexuality. Influential members of the congregation with particular and rigid theological stances may determine the acceptance or rejection of a particular preacher's message. Preachers who exhibit self-direction and an ability for self-critique appear freer in the preaching event.

What passes for preaching or good preaching varies by denomination, class, and education. The length of the sermon may be a standard fifteen minutes in a United Methodist Church and an hour in a charismatic or pentecostal church. A sermon distended with twenty-five texts and minimal exegesis may be captivating in one setting and extensive exegesis of one focus text may bring the masses to discipleship in another. A story-soaked sermon with the focus text mentioned in passing may be the model of preaching in one location and rich poetic language interwoven with the biblical story may establish one as a "great preacher" in another. In the same way, acceptable sermon topics and content vary among church cultures. Some preachers would never preach a sermon about anything political, believing that the church is not the place for politics. Other preachers believe that one is not preaching unless addressing injustice.

An essential element of sermon transportability in a variety of cultural contexts is a form of "code switching"[9] or bilingualism. That is, the speaker is able to use two or more linguistic varieties, tonal registers, dialects, or levels of language in the same conversation. The preacher is aware of the communication conventions, the role and function of acceptable language with the listeners.[10] Code switching is a learned behavior that allows members of certain cultural groups, for instance, African Americans, to move in and out of standard English in order to represent their own cultural emotional codes. Code switching reflects the culture and identity of the preacher promoting solidarity with one segment of the congregation and opening up the sermon reception with others. This is important to the emotive content of preaching. Code switching allows the preacher to manipulate, influence, or define the situation as they wish, and to convey nuances of meaning and personal intention. Repetition of a phrase, word, or idea in the language of the majority of the listeners allows the preacher to reinforce, emphasize, or clarify a point delivered in one code but will likely be misunderstood in another. New preachers should use a thesaurus in order to translate a polysyllabic word into a monosyllabic one, an academic word into vernacular, or a particular cultural expression into one for persons from a different culture. Consideration of code switching is critical in diverse multicultural churches even when everyone is of the same ethnicity.

Televangelism

One of the critical cultural phenomena influencing sermon delivery in the twenty-first century is televangelism. The increasing popularity of televangelism, Webcasts, religious conferences, international evangelistic crusades, and sale of sermonic audio and videotapes has led to linguistic patterns that have pushed stereotypical, traditional, cultural, ethnic, denominational, and sexual "sound like" boundaries. That is, congregations have access to a variety of preachers different from the local church preacher. These models often become the standard by which the listeners gauge the efficacy of the local preacher.

Televangelism or electronic preaching began in 1954 when Everett C. Parker founded the Office of Communication of the United Church of Christ to facilitate increased communication skills of ministers, activities of local churches, and to use television for education. Its predecessor, religious radio, dates back to 1927. Televangelism has morphed into a multibillion-dollar, 24/7, Webcast, tape, and DVD distribution of preaching with its own distinctive language.

When I have assigned students to view televangelists, they have described what they saw with a range of words and phrases such as flat, distant, performance, loud, energetic, the real word, techno-enhanced, evangelical, prejudiced, camera angles, theologically weak, absent exegesis, colorful, and exciting. Critiques and entertainment value not withstanding, television and Webcast sermons provide immediate and easy access to faith language. Faith objects, terminology, symbols, signs, and values are evident. Pulpits, robed choirs, the cross, altars, organs, the Bible, hymn singing, responsive interracial congregations, and powerful, convicted preachers can be found here. Media expert William A. Fore states that the preacher's robe and Bible indicate the authority that person holds. Many televangelists no longer wear robes but substitute colorful suits and dresses with diamonds and display other symbols of wealth. Celebrity preachers speak of being "favored by God" to be wealthy and claim thousands of followers. Entertainers, athletes, and politicians make guest appearance to discuss how their faith has elevated them.

Popular topics for televangelists include healing, wealth, faithfulness, obedience, patriotism, and family values. Pentecostals and charismatics spend considerable time on the gifts of the Holy Spirit, fundamentalists on doctrine and contending for the faith, and evangelicals on winning converts around the globe. Other media specialists tracking the phenomenon report the following topics being featured most frequently: God, Jesus, the Bible as a text, other uses of the Bible, sin, Satan, faith, healing, heaven, being "saved," being "born again," other religions, missionaries to foreign countries, the second coming of Christ, hell, creation, the state of Israel, missionary programs in the United States, the supernatural, Armageddon, atheism, and creationism over evolution. The preacher usually uses one or more proof texts to substantiate his or her point. Theological language most often used are phrases such as "The Bible says . . . ," "name it and claim it", "stepping into your season," "live in your purpose," "What He's done for others, He'll do for you," and "Listen, I'm about to teach you something." Personal testimony regarding the obedience of the faithful who adhere to prosperity theology predominates.[11] The Bible is the principal authority. The preacher is the prophet.

More needs to be written on the effect of televangelism on the local church and the future of preaching. How does it affect the way people in the pew listen to sermons? How does it affect the way preachers preach? Clearly, many student preachers take preaching classes are mirroring the language, style, and demeanor of televangelists. As these preachers enter full-time ministry, the effect of televangelism on local church preaching will increase.

As the religious population ages, preachers must develop visual and auditory imagery coupled with technological enhancement when available. Use of movie clips, religious art, thematic songs, manipulated handheld objects, interactive PowerPoint and computerized messages, Web camera services, hologram projections of preachers, and international interfaith conferences will continue.

Exercises for Inculturating the Word

Intercultural Understanding Exercise

Describe your perceptions of your class, colloquy group, peers:

- Composition: cultural diversity (ethnicity, race, gender, age, denomination, sexuality, health, etc.)
- Your understanding of the varied cultures (If you could ask a person of a different culture a question what would it be?)
- The preacher's authority
- What encompasses "good" preaching or expectations of the preaching moment? Should there be a preaching "norm"?
- Are there discernable differences in how your peers are responsive or involved with the preaching moment?

Exercise for understanding the congregation:

- What is the ethnic, cultural, gender, age, racial, health, theological, social, educational composition of your congregation?
- What is the "typical" worship style/form/design used?
- What comprises "good" preaching in your setting?
- How do listeners "respond" to preaching?
- How do listeners participate in worship?
- Who is listening? What is your estimation of the faith stance of the congregation? (Believers, nonbelievers, pretenders, churched, unchurched, dechurched, those in transition)

- Is your preaching transportable or adaptable?
- Are there any topics that would be off limits in this setting?

Televangelism/Web Site Exercise

The context and content of much of televised (Internet or television) preaching is:

- Self-disclosure/life story
- Authority
- Patriotism, American values
- Family
- Responsibility
- Sin
- Healing
- Necessity of personal conversion
- Spirit power
- Compassion for listener
- Use of biblical text
- Speaking in vernacular or simple "in-language"
- Ascribes roles
- Fundraising
- Music
- Prayer

In groups consider:

- What Web site or radio/TV station do you use to access televangelists?
- What televangelist attracts you most? Why?
- What televangelist do you most find problematic? Why?
- What aspects of televangelism do you emulate or seek to avoid in your preaching?

Were you to begin a television or Internet program utilizing preaching, how would you deal with the following issues:

- target audience?
- set design?
- format?
- sermon themes?
- sermon length?
- other liturgical considerations?

Were you to design a Web site for ministry, how would you deal with the following issues:

- name of site/ministry?
- focus?
- aspects of home page?
- elements of site (prayer, sermons, music, store)?

Exercises on Sermon Portability

1. In groups of two, describe the demographics of your primary preaching location (age, gender balance, ethnicity, race, socio-economic, theology, denomination, physical ability, length of membership, biblical translation used).
   a. Review you congregational information with your preaching partner (15–20 min.).
   b. Prepare a five-minute sermon based on 1 Cor. 1:26-31; Eph. 4:14-16; Exod. 12:33-42; Micah 6:6-8; or Rev. 7:9-14 for your preaching partner's setting.
   c. Following the sermon, discuss your estimation of the effectiveness of the sermon in your primary context. What works? What does not? What have you learned about your context, new ideas, what have you learned about preaching in the opposite context?
2. If you primarily preach with adults, how would you speak about war, homelessness, prejudice, death, justice, disease with children or youth?
3. If you primarily preach with persons in your own ethnic group or denomination, how would you preach the sermon in a context that is decidedly different from your own?
4. If you were assigned to preach at a women's prison, county jail, juvenile facility, hospice, military installation, what considerations would you have for sermon content and style?

Multicultural Church Exercises

Consider the following congregational context:

1. The area is multiracial, multicultural, and fast growing due to a new Internet technology complex that has drawn persons from around the globe. The area was previously undeveloped.
2. Demographics: 330 people. Church is three years old.

- Age ranges: Adults, 24–67 (235 members). Youth, birth to 17 (95 members). Median age is 40.
- Employment rate: 85 percent.
- Educational level: high school graduate 90 percent, bachelor's degree 65 percent, master's or above 45 percent, postgraduate 12 percent.
- Socioeconomic level: 75 percent middle class, 10 percent upper class.
- Family structure: blended, single parents, singles who have formed familial groups, married with children, married with no children.
- Eighteen "sandwiched" families: grandparents live with eight families with children below age ten, five parents are living with married couples without children, two are widowed parents living with a divorced child with teenage children, and three parents live with their adult children who are single, never married.
- Ethnicity: 75 percent the preacher's ethnicity, 25 percent other ethnicities.
- Health: Twenty-five of the members are admitted recovering addicts (drugs, alcohol, sex, shopping, food). Fifteen members have recently been hospitalized for coronary, diabetes, cancer, and high blood pressure problems. As the pastor you are aware that three of your members have contracted HIV, one is living with AIDS.
- Four women and one man have reported to you that they have been victims of domestic abuse.
- Three members have been incarcerated within the past three years.
- There have been approximately thirty deaths since the church began (including one suicide, one murder, one vehicular, one infant).
- About 60 percent of the persons have at some time been active church members of varying denominations, including Catholic. Another 25 percent had terrible experiences in the church due to age, gender, sexual orientation, economic standards, or theological disagreements and left their denominations. The other 15 percent have been basically unchurched—they have not had religious educations, their parents did not belong to church, they see no value in

churches, and they view the church is filled with religious hypocrites who spout community on Sunday and isolate themselves on Mondays.

3. The church is relatively new. Social ministries are being developed. About 40 percent of your congregation is active socially and politically. Twenty percent are aware of issues, will vote according to their beliefs, but are not active participants in rectifying matters. The remaining adults seem apathetic with no interest in anything but their internal church life and own community.

Following a poll of interest of the membership you develop a series of teachings and sermons addressing social, cultural, local and global issues. In groups of three design a five- to seven-minute sermon for this congregation. Compare and contrast the approaches you choose.

Chapter 3

Voicing the Word

John is a slender-built, white pastor of a congregation of approximately fifteen hundred members. He preaches three times each Sunday. He is tired physically and his voice is fatigued. He sounds lethargic, although tapes of his Sunday worship service present a vibrant, energetic, and captivating preacher. His voice is hoarse and wheezy on Tuesday morning. He complains of "losing my voice" and "I keep on clearing my throat" by the third service each Sunday. He immerses himself in the text, but the listeners in class must strain to hear him.

James is a short, well-built, African American, thirty-something man who has been preaching since he was fourteen. He is generally low-key, low-energy during class discussions, bordering on disinterest. He presents himself as a "preaching expert" who has studied all the "great preachers." He confidently moves to the podium and opens his Bible, and then a tsunami of vocal expression sweeps over the room, overpowering the ears of all in the classroom and in the hall outside the classroom. He associates powerful preaching with volume as he skirts the text but hammers home his current agenda.

Kay is an older white female who has taught Sunday school for years but only began preaching last year. She begins the sermon with a soft but effective voice that causes people to sit a bit forward to hear her. Her volume, however, increases as she engages the listeners with facial expressions, rhetorical inquiries, and associated body language. Her voice comes to fill the room but is never overwhelming. She enjoys sharing information, and although she at times sounds like she is lecturing, she exhibits no significant communication barriers during the preaching moment.

Teachers of preaching listen to countless students each year in the classroom, at conferences, and in churches. Depending on the age, gender, ethnicity, health or physicality, geographic origin, and culture of the preacher, along with the context of sermon, the preacher may have difficulty in clarity of speech as perceived by the listener or the preacher. Students have learned the process of preaching the same way preachers of the past have—"sitting at the feet" of other preachers. Some take on the pattern of their role models. Some emulate the senior pastor. Some imitate the up and coming "powerhouse evangelist." Some have to watch every televangelist they can Monday thorough Sunday so that they can "sound" like them, "really deliver the word" like them, and gain opportunities to preach—after all, one has to do what is popular so lives can be changed. The difficulty is that some preachers never find their own voice. Some develop self-identity with a subdued yet powerful voice. Others are vocally agile enough to navigate comfortably the move in and out of a principally "masculine" or "feminine" voice depending on the occasion. Some even believe that the louder you are the more powerful you are as a preacher. The level and range of the preacher's speaking voice, appropriate loudness, the distinctive quality of the preacher's voice in terms of smoothness, emotion, or tonality, "culturally accepted" vocabulary, slang, idioms, acronyms, or syntax in particular contexts determines the efficiency of the vocalization.[1] This chapter will review the importance of *voice* on the part of the preacher and *active hearing* on the part of the congregation during the preaching moment. First, voice.

Vocal Production

In the last chapter we spoke of voice metaphorically, in terms of the preacher finding her or his own voice in the pulpit. We turn now to study the literal use of voice in speech. There are three major components of voice or speech production: the breathing mechanism, the larynx, and the vocal cavities or articulators.[2]

Respiration or breathing is accomplished through the interaction of the lungs, trachea (windpipe), rib cage, and diaphragm (the muscular floor that separates the chest from the abdomen). We exchange oxygen and carbon dioxide approximately eighteen times per minute when sitting and twenty-two times per minute when standing. The most common breathing problems observed in preaching or public speaking are:

- speaking too long without a breath
- pausing only for short gasps of air
- too much neck and shoulder movement

- audible breathing, as if affected by a cold, stuffiness, or exhaustion
- decreased loudness due to fatigue, hearing loss, affect, insecurity, lack of confidence
- being ill-prepared
- excessive vocal energy manifest in speaking too loud (thus being inappropriate for feedback or hearing; creating a sense of intimidation or hostility; or done out of fear, habit, or from an inappropriate model)

Vocal audibility should be natural and effortless. Adequate breathing is essential to effective voice. Breath control is accomplished by using the correct energy when setting the vocal fold into motion. Monitoring fear, anxiety, stress, and tension in the body contribute to correct vocal energy.

While preaching about a loving, caring, forgiving, grace-filled God one's voice may feel as if cotton is clogging the throat. Other times *vocal fatigue* sets in when one is straining to be heard or is so invested in the sermon that she or he becomes exhausted. This emotional overlay may be due to hearing loss, fear, excitement, fatigue, imitation, abuse, medication, illness, or just mismanaged expectations of what a preacher should sound like. This results in harsh, strident, muffled, strained, or weak voices, all of which affect delivery and reception of the message. Some unidentifiable emotional factors also contribute to loss of voice. Each of these situations has an impact not only on vocal clarity, energy, and control but also on the perceived "power " in the message and messenger. Knowledge of the physical structures of speech production and subsequent care will help prolong one's preaching voice and decrease the cries of "I lose my voice by midday on Sunday."

Vocal Mechanism

The *larynx* (or voice box) is situated in the neck at the upper end of the trachea, and is composed of cartilage and muscles. The larynx modulates airflow with valve action of the vocal folds—soft muscle tissue approximately the size of dime—that open and close to allow air to pass from the lungs to the mouth (see fig. 3.1).[3]

The exhaled air causes the muscle tissue to vibrate producing sound. The articulators are the head, teeth, jaw, tongue, palate, and lips.

Figure 3.1 •
The Vocal Mechanism

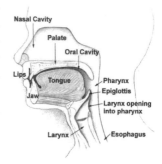

Sound vibrates and bounces across the soft moist tissue of the articulators to produce various sounds.[4] Jon Eisenson, professor of speech and language pathology, states that a voice may have acceptable characteristics and still be ineffective if the speaker's manner of producing the voice attracts attention. Through voice we share attitudes, feelings, and nuances of thought. Those listening know not only what we think, but also the essence of our feeling.[5] Eisenson developed a brief self-evaluation of voice that I have adapted for preaching:

- Is my voice pleasant to hear?
- Does my voice reflect the message I intended to convey in thought and feeling?
- Does my voice have characteristics that I would consider undesirable in another preacher?
- Does my voice reflect my personality?
- Do I want to express the pastoral or the prophetic personality?
- Is my articulation (diction) up to my own standards/expectation?
- Is my diction similar to that of my peers or listeners?
- Is there something in my voice that needs improvement?
- Are the changes in pitch, loudness, duration, and quality appropriate to the changes in thought and/or feeling that I am trying to convey?
- Would I listen to this voice if I were not the preacher?

The voice of the preacher must be appropriate to the age, gender, and physicality the listener perceives or the communication channel is disrupted. The level and range of the preacher's speaking voice, appropriate loudness, the distinctive quality of the preacher's voice in terms of smoothness, emotion, or tonality, "culturally accepted" vocabulary, slang, idioms, acronyms, or syntax in particular contexts determine the efficiency of the vocalizations.[6] One is diagnosed with a voice problem when pitch, loudness, or quality of that sound calls more attention to itself than what the preacher is saying. Vocal quality issues include hoarseness, breathiness, harshness, "lump in the throat" sound, decreased pitch range, vocal fatigue, a "scratchy" voice, and vocal roughness. These attributes may prove problematic if the congregation is not accustomed to the preacher's voice.

Sometimes the voice problem is temporary, as when preaching a number of sermons in short order or talking incessantly, or more permanent when the vocal folds either are paralyzed in an open or closed position. Sound production problems can be organic or functional. *Organic* problems include edema or swollen folds or nodules resultant from vocal abuse, hoarseness, or laryngi-tis. Over time, repeated misuse of the vocal folds results in soft, swollen spots on each vocal fold that develop into harder, callus-like growths. The nodules will become larger and more stiff the longer the vocal abuse continues. It has been noted that, for unknown reasons, vocal nodules occur more frequently in women between the ages of twenty and fifty.[7] Laryngeal growths such as vocal polyps appear on either one or both of the vocal folds and appear as a swelling or bump (like a nodule), a stalk-like growth, or a blister-like lesion (from viruses). Vocal nodules and polyps have similar symptoms and may include hoarseness, breathiness, a "rough" or "scratchy" voice, harshness, shooting pain from ear to ear, neck pain, decreased pitch range, or voice and body fatigue. Other disorders include laryngeal cancer (excessive smoking), contact ulcers, or vocal fold paralysis (neurological).

Functional voice loss (aphonia) may be attributed to vocal abuse (imita-tion of another) and psychological stress. Gastroesophageal reflux may cause polyp formation. Constant yelling or repeated hard vocal attack such as over-emphasizing particular sounds or excessive extended loudness in preaching may result in vocal fatigue, sore throat, or aphonia.[8] Vocal abuse takes many forms and may result from allergies, smoking, allergens, antihistamines, toxins, "Type A" personality (a person who is often tense or anxious), frequent throat clearing or frequent upper respiratory infections, lack of experience and asso-ciated stress, dehydration from too little water or too much acidity in one's system, caffeine, and speaking over noise due to poor amplification.

In an age of performance-oriented preachers, overwhelming schedules, nonsensical amplification, and style imitators the content of the sermon is at times lost in the sound of the preacher. Preachers, particularly women who tend to care for others and put themselves last, need to take time to rejuve-nate and care for their bodies. Excessive weight, illnesses, or medications can all affect breathing and vocal production. The preacher may also experience added stress in the preaching moment if he or she believes one's voice is not a "preacher's voice." For women, issues of authority and call may produce hesitant, weak, or inaudible "I'm not really here" or "I'm sorry to bother you," "I'm just a woman" voices. At the other end of the continuum are the "Listen to me," "I'm going to stand here until you get it," "I know I'm gifted" loud, abrasive voices. When the preacher is comfortable and assured that God has given both the call and authority one can speak in one's voice and stop masquerading. The vocal structure may not be able to sustain a style or voice heard in someone else.[9]

I refer all organic voice problems and persistent functional problems lasting more than ten days to medical or voice or speech language professionals. In particular, I advise solo pastors or those who preach multiple services to find a space for voice rest (no talking) prior to the preaching moment. The level of physical and emotional energy for preaching is affected by the number of persons on the ministerial staff. If the preacher is the sole minister she has to talk through much of the service and fatigue can easily arise. The church's level of activity may mean preaching in the morning and again in the afternoon or evening. In addition, the preacher's status, church polity, and congregational expectations may demand more preaching than in other spaces. In terms of ministry, one must consider the congregational sensitivity to the preacher. People insist on talking with the preacher before, during, and after the service. Time must be built into the day so that the preacher's voice can rest. The preacher sometimes talks nonstop on Sunday. One should, if at all possible, be on voice rest on Monday. Sound systems should be set to one level that is audible for the preacher and the listener and that does not lead to shouting.

One's preaching voice modifies over time and is a dependent on a number of variables. Different contexts place different demands on the preacher's voice. There may be more vocal stress associated with a three-night revival schedule than on a regular, Sunday-to-Sunday schedule. I remember preaching at a small church without air conditioning during a three-night Lenten revival. The church had purchased the lilies for Resurrection Sunday service the Saturday prior to the revival. Due to the heat in the building, the lilies opened and the church was filled with pollen. As soon as I entered the sanctuary, my throat began to constrict and my nose began to run. I knew that I would not be able to preach effectively so I respectfully asked the host pastor to remove the flowers from the pulpit area so I could regain some voice.

Pitch

The voice of the preacher must be appropriate to the age, gender, and physicality that the listener perceives or the communication channel is disrupted. Too often women preachers and men with higher vocal registers believe they must sound like traditional male preachers in order to gain credibility in the pulpit. The "masculine" style or sound—with bass or baritone tones, loud, energetic flourishes, hard consonant contact, and broad, pounding gestures—apparently has a "homiletical stamp of approval" as the only "real" preaching. I have a friend that says when people opine, "You don't sound like a preacher," she retorts with, "The real ones never do!" I caution women, in particular, to consider their vocal structure, breathing capacity, and the damage to their voice they can sustain from imitating others. We practice exercises of having sound content, using varied inflection patterns such as running scales, and talking about being authentic preachers. We work at finding their true *pitch*—the level of voice determined by age, gender, and vocal structure. I also advise each person to have an annual hearing evaluation in order to enunciate clearly, project the voice, and monitor both his or her own voice and the responsiveness of the listeners.

Pacing and Pauses

Eisenson stipulates that timing is everything. The rate and duration of speech expresses emotion—for instance, slow indicates sadness, fast indicates joy. The use of action verbs, the length and types of sentences used in speaking (that is, declarative, exclamatory, or interrogatory), and punctuation set the intonation of vocal production. The use of a pause in speech is an indication of control and transition.[10] The speaker may use the pause as a means of allowing the listener to catch up, integrate what has been said, or satisfy expectations of the homiletical event. At times preachers are reticent to pause. They feel the need to fill a void, resort to repetitions, or fear waiting even briefly for the communication to be transmitted. The pause, however, indicates the completion of a thought, timing for vocal variety, maintenance of interest, and allowing the listener to reconnect or attend to the content of the message.[11]

Tonality

Eisenson posits that the vocal variation or intonation gives melody to speech, similar to discreet musical note shifts. The melody of speech is determined in the mood, emotion, intonation, and flavor of the voice of the speaker. Better speakers produce speech in a range of one-and-one-half octaves of rising and falling of stressed syllables. Monotone speakers produce a one-half octave in expression of feelings and belief.[12] The upward and downward shift of the voice colors speech and energizes the message. Lack of movement yields a flat-sounding voice or a monotone.

Rate

Rate or fluency is the speed of vocal production—too fast, too slow, or variable. Fluency disorders disrupt the flow of speech. The preacher may be speaking at such a rapid rate that clarity of speech is sacrificed. We read faster than we speak. Manuscript-bound preachers do not sense the listener's frustration in keeping up with them. Anxiety, time constraints, natural speaking rate, fatigue, resistance to preaching, control, manipulation, and disengagement with the listener may be causative factors for having inappropriate rate. Prolongation of sounds and repetition of phrases are hallmarks of African American and charismatic preaching. These elements are viewed as dysfluencies when the listener becomes fixated on the syllable or sound the preacher has difficulty enunciating. This becomes even more problematic when the preacher clutters or stutters. There is a visible lack of control with associated physical tension, eye blinks, tapping, and head turns.[13]

Normal dysfluencies may be termed *stuttering*. The preacher repeats syllables or words once or twice: *b-b-b-ball* or *li-li-like*. In a part-word repetition the preacher may have difficulty moving from, for instance, the "wh" in "where" to the remaining sounds in the word. After several attempts the speaker may successfully complete the word, *basket-basket-basket— basketball*. In sound prolongation the preacher has difficulty moving from, for example, the "s" in "save" to the remaining sounds in the word. She continues to say the "s" sound until she is able to complete the word, *ssssss-avior*. Sometimes the preacher uses a series of interjections as if he is unable to remember the word. These dysfluencies may also include hesitancies and the use of fillers, such as "uh," "er," and "um" until the word is smoothed over or recalled. The preacher may exhibit related behaviors such as tension in the jaw or tremors in the lips or tongue while trying to preach. Dysfluencies differ from person to person and may or may necessitate professional intervention. Stuttering, however, is demonstrated as abnormal or excessive dysfluency. Causative factors for stuttering range from genetics to child development to neurophysiology to family dynamics.[14] The preacher who stutters may try to mask their dysfluency by circumlocution or rearranging the words in their sentences, pretending to forget what they wanted to say, or declining to speak. She may appear to be very tense or "out of breath" when talking. His speech may become completely stopped or blocked leading to frustration and at times congregants trying to fill in the words or to look away as not to embarrass the preacher.

Musicality

Homiletician William Turner writes about intensity in preaching. He states that Christian preaching is an attempt to account for its transcendence over ordinary speech. One preaches "outside of the self" on behalf of the divine presence with more affective and emotional than reflective and intellectual voice. The preacher's use of musicality is the linguistic intonation, ebb and flow, call and response, inflection and physicality inherent in many forms of black and charismatic preaching. It often evokes and expresses the emotional content of the sermon.[15] Musicality in the preaching event need not be limited to the preacher. Evans Crawford details the "homiletical musicality" or audible responses from the congregation during the preaching moment. In black preaching the exchange is known as call and response. Crawford examines five possible responses—*Help 'em, Lord!*, *Well?*, *That's all right!*, *Amen!*, and *Glory Hallelujah!*—to the preacher's vocalized and at times physical message. In communication theory it is a vocal feedback loop of sender-message-receive-sender. It is an exchange of information between preacher and people, based on cultural experience, freedom of artistic and linguistic expression, and a belief in spiritual endowment that resonates between the preacher and the listener. The representative listener's response actually helps the preacher assess how the congregation is receiving the message. Crawford says that timing, pauses, inflection, pace, and the musical qualities of speech engage the listener during proclamation.[16] I posit that call and response may be vocal or nonvocal, verbal or nonverbal. The preacher may clap his hands and the congregation may imitate the move. The congregation may stand up and move around as the preacher beings to shift from behind the podium. This is a nonvocal call and response or musicality. These musical elements are used by men and women, across ethnicities, ages, and cultures.

Some of the qualities of musicality are intonation, rhythm, and repetition. *Intonation* is described as having a musical quality using sustained tones. In some cultures impromptu songs, folk tales, wisdom fables, and inspirational sayings are intoned in a natural, free-flowing voice. I require students to take turns opening the class with prayer and song in order to instill practice in intonation. Even the tone-deaf and monotone show some improvement. Use of *rhythm* provides breaks for breaths and makes room for response. Rhythm contributes to the flow of the sermon. Preachers are encouraged to slow down to allow their listeners to process the content when the sermon content contains questions. Overall the speed of delivery in musicality is dependent on the verbal ability of the preacher, the reception rate of the listener, the inherent cultural dynamics, the sermon form, the illustrations or supportive content, and expectation of what passes for good preaching. *Repetition* is the restatement of sound, word, or phrase for emphasis. It is a means to instill something into people's memory. Repetition is used for impact, for effect. Some preachers present a vocalized stammer. It is a repetition of part of a word or blocking on sound production that builds intensity, cause people to attend to what comes next. This stammer is practiced and may entail a cultural genre in black preaching in particular that is used for linguistic effect.

The level and range of the preacher's speaking voice, appropriate loudness, the distinctive quality of the preacher's voice in terms of smoothness, emotion, or tonality, "culturally accepted" vocabulary, slang, idioms, acronyms, or syntax in particular contexts determine the efficiency of the vocalizations. Some of the voice and diction elements that have a direct impact on the clarity of preaching voice and uninterrupted transmission are:

a. Voice Quality—volume, pitch, nasality, intensity, projection
b. Breathing/Respiration Pattern (sustaining air flow)—breathy, clavicular, diaphragmatic, impediments (asthma, sinus, cold, medications, etc.)
c. Articulation/Phonation (sound production)—tongue mobility, lips, jaw, teeth, palate
d. Fluency—use of pauses, cluttering, stuttering, rate
e. Posture—alignment, use of hands, use of eyes, associated nonverbal cues
f. Dialect—regional, ethnic, cultural, nationality

Those who exhibit voice and breathing problems, raspy or harsh voice, inaudibility, loudness problems, pitch breaks, ineffective pausing, or nonverbal disengagement with the listener or the sermon content should receive a cursory voice and diction evaluation based on the list above. Preachers should both audiotape and videotape themselves monthly. If professional taping equipment is not available, a voice-activated tape recorder will suffice. Although it may be difficult to accept, those who listen to preachers routinely either adapt to misarticulation, ignore the sounds, or provide blistering critiques of the preacher's voice and diction. Referrals to speech and language professionals, hearing specialists, or voice teachers are suggested for students with major organic or structural complications.

⊕ Exercises for Voicing the Word

All preachers need to be concerned with their vocal health and can use voice and diction exercises for this purpose. Such voice and organics or structural diction exercises can also be used to address specific functional or manageable problems. The problem, of course, is that many of us are unaware we have a speech problem unless someone, usually a professional (such as a professor in a homiletics course), points it out. As noted above, preachers should analyze audio and video recordings of their sermons for voice and diction clarity.

Preaching Voice and Diction Evaluation Sheet

The following is a checklist of issues related to voice and diction that can change depending on your health, energy, medications, mental state, emotion, or volition. These broad suggestions may be used to maintain a healthy preaching voice:

1. *Illness*: If you have sinus trouble, hay fever, laryngitis, a cold, deep emotion stress, or fatigue, speak softer or go on vocal rest unless there is an emergency. Do not whisper, as it places as much stress on the vocal mechanism as normal conversational speech. Avoid prolonged speaking and yelling. If the condition persists for more than two weeks consult a doctor.

2. *Respiration*: After taking a deep breath, count slowly, one second per number, in a good loud voice. Repeat until you can count aloud to fifteen slowly on one breath. Work up until you are able to count to twenty or thirty.

   Another exercise is to sound the vowel /ah/ in a full voice and prolong it in a monotone until you feel like all the breath is exhausted. Time each trial. When taking a breath place your hand lightly on your abdomen. *Diaphragmatic breathing* means that your stomach distends when air is taken in. If your shoulders move up (*clavicular breathing*) and your stomach goes in, you are breathing incorrectly and will have minimal airflow.

3. *Posture*: Shoulders should incline slightly forward when speaking. Carriage of the chest and collarbones is relatively high. Your chin should be inclined forward, slightly, but not tucked under. Feet should be approximately ten to twelve inches apart. Exaggerated, stiff, military posture decreases vocal efficiency.

4. *Tight or tense jaw*: If you speak with little mouth opening or you clench your teeth, try chewing exercises. Pretend you have caramel or your favorite gooey food item in your mouth. Open your mouth as wide as possible and chew twenty times. With your mouth wide open, cough dryly and lightly five times. Alternate between the exercises a few times, resting in between each. You might try slow neck rolls also—first clockwise, then counterclockwise five times each. Phonate /m/ softly as you roll the head slowly, thinking of some pleasant event or place.

5. *Volume, intensity, and projection*: Remember the respiration exercise above in which we sounded the vowel /ah/. A variation of this exercise will help you work on volume. Prolong the /ah/ softly at a normal pitch level. Gradually increase the loudness of the sound /ah/ in a monotone as long as the breath

lasts. Make sure you increase the sound gradually, imagining that a person is walking away from you. Try to reach with your voice—twenty feet. If you feel a tickling, cough, or hoarseness you are overstraining. Stop if this occurs. Next decrease the volume as if the person is walking toward you. Always direct your voice toward the person. Once you master this distance without strain, try thirty, forty, and fifty feet. Also, vary the exercise by having inflection patterns go up and down as well as monotone, /ah–h/.

6. *Fluency and rate*: Speak as rapidly as you wish, as long as you articulate all speech sounds. When you seem to produce numerous pauses and repetitions of words or sounds or you can't seem to produce the next word without struggle, your dysfluencies are termed *stuttering*. If you speak so rapidly that your speech is generally incoherent or words seem to be connected into one long sentence your dysfluencies are termed *cluttering*.

    An average reading rate is 135 to 175 words per minute; often preachers use this as his or her speaking rate. The preacher must consider the hearing patterns of the listener. Some persons process information slower, others faster. Variety in rate is essential to the audibility of the sermon. The mood, style, and situation of the speaker determine the speed of presentation. As you vary your rate maintain easy breathing, clear voice production, incisive articulation, proper phrasing, pausing, and inflection.

    a. Practice reading prose or poetry using a voice recorder. First read at your normal rate, then read faster, then slower. Listen to the tape and compare your clarity at the different speeds. Have someone else listen to the tape and rate your clarity— they will catch things you miss.

    b. Read the passage allowing two beats between each word. Use a rate of sixty to one hundred syllables (*not* words) per minute. Prolong the vowel sound in each syllable. Practice with the twenty-foot volume projection. Attend to the articulation of each sound.

Hearing and Listening

Preaching not only involves the preacher's voice but also the preacher's and the listener's ears. Oral competence is grounded in the intentions of the speaker and receptivity of the listeners as they seek to know what the preacher thinks or feels. Speech communication includes sounds, gestures, events, and people. Craig Loscalso speaks of identification with the listener as means of preacher-congregation linguistic unit.[17] One of the primary complaints about sermons is that they are boring, flat, uninspired, irrelevant, and unintelligible. At times sermon transmission is disrupted by muffled and masked sounds. Sometimes the listener does not hear anything the preacher says not because he or she does not want to hear but because there is a distinctive loss of hearing. The preacher may not articulate words clearly because of his own hearing loss.

Hearing is a physical act involving the mechanical and neurological reception of sensory impulse of sound in outer ear, middle ear, and inner ear. See the following diagram (fig. 3.2).[18]

Hearing is the reception of sound through sensory fluctuations of air pressure. More precisely, it is the process of translating these fluctuations into an electrical signal that the brain can understand and interpret as distinct sounds arranged into an auditory amalgamation of syllables, words, phrases, sentences, and paragraphs.

Listening is active hearing. We spend approximately 45 percent of our time in active listening. However, 70 percent of oral communication is misunderstood, ignored, or quickly forgotten. The elements of listening are sensing or hearing the message, understanding what is said, evaluating the information, and responding to what is heard by doing something or storing information for future use.[19] The two major categories of hearing impairment are sensorineural and conductive.

Sensorineural hearing loss occurs when there is damage to the inner ear (cochlea) or to the nerve pathways from the inner ear (retrocochlear) to the brain. Sensorineural hearing loss cannot be medically or surgically corrected. It is a permanent loss. Sensorineural hearing loss not only involves a reduction in sound level or ability to hear faint sounds, but also affects speech understanding or ability to hear clearly. Sensorineural hearing loss can be caused by diseases, birth injury, drugs that are toxic to the auditory system, and genetic syndromes. Sensorineural hearing loss may also occur as a result of noise exposure, viruses, head trauma, aging, and tumors. A sensorineural hearing loss, on the other hand, mostly affects hearing acuity in the high frequency range. The high-pitched speech sounds (such as /s/, /f/, /sh/, /t/) play a crucial role in our ability to understand speech clearly. This is why a person with a sensorineural loss will often say, "I can hear but often I don't understand what is said."

Conductive hearing begins with conditions associated with middle ear pathology such as fluid in the middle ear from colds, allergies (serous otitis media), poor eustachian tube function, ear infection (otitis media), perforated eardrum, benign tumors, impacted earwax (cerumen), infection in the ear canal (external otitis), presence of a foreign body in the ear canal, or the absence or malformation of the outer ear, ear canal, or middle ear. A conductive hearing loss usually results in a hearing deficiency in the low frequency range. That is, the low-pitched sounds (deep sounds such as /o/, /u/) that provide a lot of the "volume" of speech are affected the most. This lowers the loudness of the incoming speech signal but does not affect its clarity.

Figure 3.2 • The Ear Mechanism

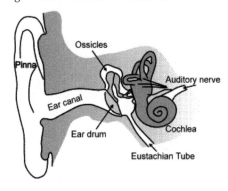

In sermonic discourse the listener should be able to recognize the premise, associate it to past experience, identify the premise by references to the historical or invented examples, and draw conclusions from presented information. Emphatic listening provides maximum understanding of the speaker's intent and content. The listener evaluates through deliberative or selective listening. The emphatic listener recalls critical issues, agreements, or disagreements with the speaker and draws conclusions. The deliberative listener may have minimal understanding and is predisposed to criticize, summarize, conclude, agree, or disagree.[20] With the maturing of society, more and more of our congregants will suffer some form of hearing loss. The constant barrage of speakers, microphones, exposure to viruses, allergens, aging, and fatigue will ultimately not only effect hearing but also voice production. I suggest that preachers have hearing tests as part of their annual physicals. If the preacher is unable to assess her voice or notes there is some difficulty in hearing there are a number of professionals, such as speech-language and hearing pathologists, who will assist in assessment and treatment.

Preaching is a sacred oral-aural event. Attention to speech production and speech perception is essential for enhanced communication. The loss or poor production of voice or hearing will diminish the efficacy of the sermon.

⚙ More Voice Exercises

Discovering Your Own Voice Exercise

Answer the following questions:

- Who are your preaching parents or role models?
- Who is in the "company of preachers" with whom you regularly associate?
- Do you sing, read or write poetry, or play an instrument?
- What type of music do you listen to most often?
- What is your "preaching signature"? What type of voice is most characteristic of your preaching?
- If you could modify anything about your voice, what would it be?
- How often do you listen to a recording of your voice?

Review the following questions and begin to formulate means for affirming your own voice in personal relationships, seminary, home, church, and community. (The questions are a blend of suggestions found in Lee McGee, *Wrestling with the Patriarchs: Retrieving Women's Voices in Preaching* (Nashville: Abingdon, 1996) and my work as a speech-language pathologist.)

- Think of two or three situations in which you use or do not use your voice. Why?
- What or who inhibits the use of your voice?
- Do you believe you listen more attentively to men's or to women's voices? Why?
- What are the "cultural" variables or situations that reinforce resistance to particular voices?
- In what situations or places do you feel you receive most encouragement to use your voice?
- In what ways do you resist hearing women's or men's voices?
- Is there a particular voice that you enjoy listening to and why?
- Describe the sound of your own voice? After each person in the group has shared, describe the sound of the voices of the persons in your group. Speaking metaphorically may be most helpful, for instance, "Your voice sounds like cotton, sand paper, a whisper . . ."
- What do you like most about your voice?
- Is there anything about your voice that you want to change? If so, what?

- What is the source of the most tension for you in the preaching moment?
- Do you currently use tension-releasing methods prior to or during the preaching moment?

The following exercise can also help a preacher identify her or his unique preaching voice. First think of the last two or three sermons you preached. Then use these questions (based on David Schlafer's *Your Way with God's Word: Discovering Your Distinctive Preaching Voice* [Cambridge: Cowley, 1995])[21] to help you think about your preaching voice in new ways:

- What is the color of your preaching?
- How does it look?
- How does your preaching smell?
- How does it sound?
- How does it feel? (if you were able to touch it)
- If the sermon were a meal, how would it taste?

Biblical Expression of Voice Exercise
Take about fifteen minutes to prepare a three- to five-minute sermon.

- Preach *only* from the selected text.
- Avoid clichés, think about how voice is expressed in the biblical text.

Selected texts on silence/voice/tongue/proclaiming:

- *Old Testament*: Ecclesiastes 3:7; Psalm 94:17; Psalm 32:3; Proverb 12:19; Proverb 18:21
- *New Testament*: 1 Peter 2:15; Mark 7:33; Matthew 10:7; 1 Corinthians 1:17; 1 Corinthians 14:10; Philippians 2:11

Auditory Exercise

Perform this exercise in small groups or individuals may tape their responses. The task is to describe certain nouns used often in preaching as sounds. There are no wrong answers other than dull descriptions.

- If you could hear God's voice how would it sound?
- Choose and describe the sound(s) of one of the listed words: peace, hate, love, disappointment, healing, joy, hunger, relief, resurrection
- Select a text and prepare a three- to five-minute sermon focusing on the word and sounds. The intent is for preachers to practice auditorally connecting with listeners as well as deepening imagery in sermons. The preacher is able to "listen" to his or her own voice and make modifications to intonation that does not express the sound, emotion, impact of the specified words.

Chapter 4

Articulating the Word

Martin grew up in middle Georgia. He is a senior pastor of a charismatic, evangelical church with twelve years of experience. His idiosyncrasies include a heavy drawling dialect marked by slow, deliberate speech, pronunciation of "mirruh" for "mirror," omission of "ing" at the end of words, "y'all" for "you all" or "you," "git" for "get," "oughta" for "ought to" and substitution of "got to" or "gottuh" for "have." His presence and articulation are almost a caricature of media representations of southern white men. His sincerity and reverence for preaching, however, opens the way for effective communication in spite of how northern listeners perceive his dialectic.

Charles is a tall, average-built man who walks with militaristic bearing. His face is serious, rarely cracking a smile even in laughter. He articulates his belief that preaching is a life-and death-matter with little place for humor or excessive movement. His pronunciation is precise and follows midwestern or standard American English, reflecting his Nebraska upbringing. He experiences difficulty attending to the speech of the other preachers, often critiquing their pronunciation of such words as "improper," "ethnic," or "lazy."

Richelle creates words as she preaches, mispronounces biblical names, uses only language from the King James translation, and prolongs or distorts words such as "God" (Gahd or Goooodu), "Jesus" (Jeezuz), "Lord" (Lourd or Laard, depending on the day or audience) or "Bible" (Bahble or Biiible). Her style is fast-paced with varied inflections, punctuated with jargon and clichés, and at times ear-splitting in volume. She runs back and forth across the front of the classroom in frantic excitement. She also has a regular televised sermon show on a local public access channel.

Each of these preachers models a distinctive way to communicate their message. Their effectiveness depends on their intelligibility. The specialized use of the vocal mechanism in speaking and singing must be afforded particular attention in sermon delivery. One's ability to communicate a message clearly and effectively is directly affected by the type of voice and diction one possesses. This chapter will present in formation on basic articulation, phonation, intonation, mood, flavor, color, quality, tone, clarity, dialect, and vernacular.

Sound Production: Articulation and Phonation

In the last chapter we examined the vocal mechanism in our discussion of vocal production and vocal problems. Let us expand on that discussion now as look at specific details of phonation and articulation. *Phonation* is the production of sound that occurs when your vocal folds vibrate as air coming up from the lungs passes between them. *Articulation,* on the other hand, involves the further modification of that air stream through the manipulation of your lips, tongue, teeth, jaw, palate, and bronchial tube. It is important that we who spend so much of our careers dedicated to speech to have some familiarity with the technical details of sound production (technical terms are presented in *italics*), because understanding the many ways we combine phonation and articulation techniques will help us speak with better clarity from the pulpit.

Voiced and Unvoiced Sounds

Basic American English sounds/phonemes are divided into voiced and unvoiced sounds. The *vocal folds* are a pair of muscular flaps in the throat that can be brought together to form a seal, or opened to permit airflow. The basic sound produced by vocal-fold vibration is called *voiced* sound. When the vocal folds are not made to vibrate, the sound is described as *unvoiced.* Sound that passes through the vocal folds is amplified and modified by the *vocal tract resonators* (the throat, mouth cavity, and nasal passages). The same type of manipulation of vocal tract resonators creates different sounds depending on whether the sound is voiced or unvoiced. Produce the sounds in the following list. With each pair notice how you are using the vocal tract resonators in the same way, but hold your hand to your throat to feel the difference in vibration between the sound that is voiced and the one that is not:

Unvoiced	Voiced
s	z
f '	v
p	b
k	g

Sounds are further divided into vowels and consonants based on which artic-ulators are used to produce them. First, vowels. Although we generally speak of the vowels as "a, e, i, o, u, and sometimes y," there are many more vowel sounds in the English language. Each of these letters used in spelling has multiple sounds associated with them in speech. The vowel sounds are shaped by the placement of the tongue in the oral cavity. Read the words in the following list (fig. 4.1) out loud and attend to the way your tongue changes shape from word to word.

Figure 4.1

/i/ /ee/	wheat	/uh/	but
/i/ /iy/	pit	/uw/ /uy/	boot
/eh/	bet	/uh/	cup
/a/ (ey)	stable	/uh/	foot
/ah / (ae)	cattle	/oy/	boy
/a/	candle	/ah/ (@)	about
/aw/ (au)	father	/ ah / (aa)	potter
/er/	hurry	/oh/ (ow)	boat

Place of Articulation

The resonators we have been discussing produce a person's recognizable voice. Place of articulation specifies where the sound is made. There is more variety in the way we shape consonants. The list of articulators given below (fig. 4.2) demonstrates the range. Pronounce the words offered as examples out loud and feel how the place of articulation varies.

Articulation Problems

There are times when the preacher fails to produce sounds in a manner reso-nant with the culture, geography, or common usage. *SODA* is an acronym used in speech-language pathology for types of misarticulations (Substitution,

Figure 4.2 • Articulators

Bilabial (two lips) lips pressed together	/p/ pay /b/ baby
Nasal-bilabial lips pressed together and air forces into nasal cavity	/m/ manna
Glide-bilabial lips slightly open in "o" and air moving over tongue	/w/ will, wise /hw/ what, wheel
Lip-teeth fricative or *Labiodental* lower lip + upper teeth lips slightly open, tensed, teeth touching or almost touching	/v/ very /f/ faith
Tongue-hard palate *Palatal:* body of the tongue raised to the palatal region	/r/ reverence redemption
Glottal at the larynx (space between vocal folds) mouth open, sound produced in back of throat	/h/ high hand

Tongue-soft palate *Velar*: back of the tongue raised to soft palate (velum) tongue moves up touching rear of roof of the mouth	/g/ God, give /h/ heaven, hell /ng/ praying, loving
Tongue-teeth fricative *Interdental*: tongue between or just behind the upper teeth tongue protrudes between teeth; or tongue touches behind upper teeth ridge	/th/ theology /th/ the, that
Alveolar tongue tip at the alveolar ridge tongue touches the roof of mouth or just behind gum line	/d/ die /t/ today /z/ zeal /s/ savior /ch/ church /sh/ sheep /n/ now /l/ lean /j/ joy
Blends combinations of movements producing sound	/bl/ bless /pl/ plea /spl/ splendor /pr/ pray /gr/ great /sk/ sky /tr/ try

Omissions, Distortion, Addition). Preachers can use it as a reminder to work on articulation errors in the pulpit.

1. *Substitution*—substituting one sound for another similar sound
     Common substitutions: d/th; f/th; w/r; b/v; w/y
     Examples: /f/ for /th/ ("fum" for "thumb"); /l/ for /y/ ("lelo" for "yellow"); /w/ for /r/ ("wabbit" for "rabbit"); /th/ for /s/ ("thun" for "sun")

2. *Omission*—dropping a letter or sound from a word, usually (but not always) from the end of the word
     Commons omissions: /ing/, /ed/, /s/
     Examples: "stopped" becomes "stop," "window" becomes "winow," "fish" becomes "fi," "at" for "cat," "eain" for "eating"

3. *Distortion*—the intended sound is incorrectly pronounced
     Common distortion: Lisps (lateral or bilateral) are evident in people who are unable to pronounce sounds like /s/ or /z/ and replace them with sounds like /th/. The result is a sound like air escaping or hissing from the mouth.
     Examples: "shlip" for "sip," "thaw" for "saw," "thobathun" for "salvation"

4. *Addition*—extra syllables or sounds are added to a word, usually in the initial or middle position of words
     Examples: "cuhlean" for "clean," "Goda" for "God," "animamal" for "animal"

A combination of substitutions, omissions, distortions, and additions may be evident in sermons. Depending on the listener's hearing ability and level of active listening, they may interfere with receiving the content of the sermon.

The listener may attend more to how the person is speaking than what is being said. The preacher must take seriously any problems that diminish the intelligibility of what she or he is trying to communicate.

Misarticulation can have numerous causes. They may result from brain damage or neurological dysfunction, physical handicaps, such as cerebral palsy, cleft palate, or hearing loss. The condition may be related to lack of coordination of the movements of the mouth, even dental problems. Sometimes choosing alternative words for those that preachers have physical difficulty articulating works wonders for improved clarity. Some of the overarching speech problems resulting from physical problems can be improved with the aid of a specialist.

Most articulation problems preachers experience, however, occur in the absence of any obvious physical disability. They are instead *functional articulation problems*, or learned behaviors. These do not include variations in speech patterns due to cultural and regional dialects (see below). We are speaking, instead, of preachers who experienced some speech disorder as children and did not receive corrective procedures, perhaps because it was too mild to be noticed. But as a public speaker, preachers need to attend to such problems. Some listeners rate a preacher's formal education or seriousness on how well she or he speaks. For example, they may unconsciously confuse articulation problems with a lower level of vocabulary.

The following is a selected list of mispronounced words often heard in public speaking (fig. 4.3). Preachers should attend to any of these they do and unlearn the behavior:

Figure 4.3 • Commonly Mispronounced Words

aks	ask	liberry	library
Old-timer's disease	Alzheimer's disease	ofen	often
athelete, atheletic	athlete, athletic	perogative	prerogative
bidness	business	perscription	prescription
calvary	cavalry	probly, prolly	probably
close	clothes	piture	picture
drownd	drown	prostrate	prostate
expecially	especially	revelant	relevant
febyuary	February	supposably, susppose	supposedly, suppose
hi-archy	hierarchy	statsistick	statistic
irregardless	regardless	take for granite	take for granted
idn't	isn't	vegtable	vegetable
jist nor dis	just	wadn't	wasn't

A particular articulation problem that occurs often in the pulpit and is completely unavoidable is the mispronunciation of biblical names and locations.

Such errors are due less to physical or functional causes and more to incomplete sermon preparation. Preachers should have in their library a self-pronouncing or phonetic Bible, thesaurus, or use one of the electronic programs for correct pronunciation of Greek, Hebrew, Latin, or English words (for example, http://www.biblespeech.com, William O. Walker's *Harper's Bible Pronunciation Guide*, or http://bible.crosswalk.com/Lexicons/). And they should practice the entire sermon prior to preaching to identify and correct any areas where avoidable articulation problems might arise.

Dialects

To a great degree, one's ethnicity, nationality, culture, region, district, class, and gender defines one's manner of speaking. This is what is meant by *dialect*, a system within a system of speech. Dialects possess their own variations of pronunciation, vocabulary, grammar, syntax, and common expression. The enunciation of words such as *roof, class, burn, bury, vehicle, marry, after,* and *Missouri* is decidedly different depending on one's geographical location. Dialects may or may not interfere with the reception of the preached word depending on the social location of the listeners. In my move from Colorado to Georgia, I cringed when a preacher said "we be" (we are), "suhpuhlhker" (sepulcher), "Geeduh" (Jesus), axs (ask), "dem" (them), "heben" (heaven), "done gone" (went), "ekspecshal" (especially), or irregardless (regardless). But I have, eventually, come to use "y'all" or "you all" in place of the plural of "you."

Some strive to rise above dialects. They argue for the use of standard English as normative language and speech, as it reflects the usage of the "educated" or "proper" class. In orality, specifically, the midwestern American English dialect is the model for broadcast English, speech "without an accent" or flat dialect. But understanding and appreciating the dialect of one's hearers is an important part of preaching.

Some sources argue that there are three primary American English dialects—Northern, Midland, and Southern.[1] Others list more than thirty dialects and subdialects in American English.[2] Due to the transitory nature of contemporary society, dialects are evolving and multiplying. Humans have a tendency to reiterate sounds and words they consciously and subconsciously pick up in normal conversation, listening to music, watching movies, reading, or traveling. A representative sample of dialects helpful for preachers who receive calls outside their region of origin follows (fig. 4.4).

Moving to smaller subgroups than defined by region, specific racial ethnic groups may use a dialect within a dialect. Some examples include Black English, Ebonics, Pidgin English, Gullah, French Creole, Appalachian, Yiddish, Pennsylvania Dutch (Germanic), Cajun, Hispanic- or Asian-influenced language with English.

Figure 4.4 • Dialects

DIALECT	REGION	EXAMPLE
Northern	New England	dropped "r" or added "r' with vowel: "remebuh"; /a/ becomes /ah/: "Hahvard"
	New York City	"r" becomes a vowel: /ir/ becomes /oi/; *girl* is "goil" and *oil* is "erl"; /d/ substitutes /th/: dey for they, tirdy for thirty
Southern	General, South Midland, Ozark, Smokey Mountain, Gulf Southern, Virginia Piedmont	boogerman, jump the borrm, mammy; /a/ for /ing/: gonna for going; mouth harp (harmonica) Let down or heist up (opening or closing a window) fixin' to (going to), bad mouth (curse), juju (magic) yam (sweet potato), Nawlins (New Orleans), dawgs (dogs)
Western	Rocky Mountain, Pacific Northwest, Southwestern, Pacific Southwestern, Hawaiian	bushed (tired), kicked off (to die), belly up, bronco, ramada, plaza, mesa, mustang, roundup, "gag me", ukulele, aloha
Midwestern	Nebraska, Missouri, St. Louis, Chicago, Upper Midwestern	/r/ in ferry, furry, /eh/ in Mary-marry-merry merger (same pronunciation); faucet (spigot), pop (soda), tetertotter (seesaw)

Narrowing even further it is important to note that no two persons speak exactly the same way. In what is known as an *idiolect*, one's articulation, phrasing, rhythm, and inflection is her or his verbal "fingerprint." For preachers, both recognizing and shaping our idiolect is part of discovering one's unique voice. An idiolect is personal language, often melding of the varieties of cultures the preacher has encountered through work, education, leisure, or religion. Some people are like sponges and pick up language and speech wherever they go and from whomever they meet. I catch myself at times using a word or phrase that I heard in class from younger students, lyrics in a gospel song, faculty discussion, a catchphrase in a movie, a line of poetry, or some God-talk I picked up when reviewing sermons on the Internet. I pronounce words just as I hear them. My speech is multilevel language and multisound or a distinctive idiolect. I also pronounce sounds and words differently based on my conversation partner. For example, I would avoid saying "my girl" (my best friend), "yah" (you), or whatchat (what are you) at work but use them at home. Preachers should not hide their idiolect but should recognize that there is an appropriate difference between their private and public speech. Even though many of us seek a conversational tone in the pulpit, it is a formal speaking occasion, and our speech should reflect that.

A final note related to dialect. Words go in and out of popular usage. There is an annual revision of "new" words and outdated language. One of the biggest diction mistakes is for a preacher to use a word that is dated or mispronounce a word they believe is still popular (for example, "Wazz-up?" for "What's up?"). Preachers who think they know slang or words used by a different culture, such as a younger age group, can create a disconnect instead of the deeper connection for which they were hoping. Misarticulation can even lead to laughter or stunned silence, at which point the message may be lost. In order for the preacher to keep language fresh, she must constantly review and filter sermonic materials for dialect, vernacular, and idiolect.

Rate and Intonation

Preachers often misstate sounds in the move from reading the manuscript or sermon notes to speaking the sermon. Sometimes this can be caused by a typographical error in the manuscript—for instance, we pronounce the word as it is misspelled instead of how it really sounds. This can be avoided with careful proofreading and using the spell check in the word-processor software you use.

More often, however, misarticulation in the move from what lies on the pulpit to what is spoken over the pulpit has to do with the difference in writing and reading written discourse and speaking for the oral-aural setting. I noted earlier that there are different *rates of speaking* for reading and speaking. The more rapid the speech the more likely one is to misarticulate a word or sound.

Correct articulation can make or break the communication chain. Fortunately, many listeners overlook poor pronunciation and attend to the content. Some are stalled on one sound or word. Consider the context of preaching when deciding how to pronounce a word or use a phrase. If I know a Southern preacher will be preaching to people who use the same dialect I note the pronunciations as a dialect or regionalism. If others in the class are having difficulty understanding the person then I might address the diction. Practice the words of the biblical text prior to reading in public. The preacher's initial speech-act sets the stage for expectation of articulation in the entire sermon. One mispronounced word will be a slight distraction. Consistent misarticulation may be the "deal breaker."

⊕ Exercises for Articulating the Word in the Preaching Moment

Determining Your Sound (Idiolect)

Consider for yourself or discuss with a small group or preaching partner what represents different regional, ethnic, and cultural dialects:

1. Where did you grow up?
2. What languages were spoken around you?
3. How many languages do you speak?
4. What language did your parents speak?
5. How may countries have you visited?
6. How many states/regions have you visited?
7. Do you have friends (peers, colleagues, congregants) who say sounds or words differently than you do? Is that a barrier in conversation? Why? Why not?

8. How much of conversation is based on understood intention, and what role does dialect play in expressing intention?
9. Is there a dialect you have difficulty listening to? That you avoid? Why?
10. What is the ethnic makeup of your congregation? What expressions of dialect do you find in the group?
11. Is there a particular person whose voice you admire? Why? Have you found yourself imitating her or his speech?
12. Record your voice and briefly describe you voice and idiolect.

Poetry

Poetry is rich in inflection, imagery, wordplay, and dialect. Bring your favorite poem to class. Memorize it. Each person should take turns reciting his or her poem as others listen to the flow, pronunciation, and clarity. Discuss the way elements of performance like rate of speaking and intonation influence the hearing of the poem.

Select a biblical text that relates to the poem. Prepare a five-minute sermon using part or all of the poem as an illustration. Discuss how the performance of the poem is influenced by the sermonic context and vice versa.

Music and Preaching

The melody of music parallels the flow of speech. People who listen to rap or hip-hop speak with a different cadence than those who listen to jazz or classical pieces. The rhythms of the music infuse the physical movement when one is listening or singing. Many people remember the words or lyrics in a song easier than spoken words. In the biblical text the speech-flow of the psalms is different from the flow of the history, narratives, or wisdom literature. In preaching the tonality, color, fluency, emotion, pausing, and embodiment of the word may be improved by singing passages using the music one listens to most often. The preacher should also consider the types of music the congregation listens to most often. Matching the speech in the sermon with the listening habits of the congregation will provide one means of solidifying a connection in the feedback loop.

Music and preaching considerations

- What type of music do you listen to most?
- What does your congregation listen to most often?
- What words in songs do you detect in the conversations in the church/classroom?

- Select your favorite song-recording, lyrics, or your own vocal rendition. Sing along with the music and note the variation in inflection, emphasis, word pronunciation, jargon, cliché, emotion from your normal speech pattern.
- Listen to a genre of music that you generally avoid and discuss the pronunciation of select words. What variations would you make in your speech pattern to present a sermon with children? youth? elders? culture?
- Select a psalm. Given your musical tastes how would you sing the psalm?
- Speak the psalm using the inflection of jazz, pop, blues, traditional gospel, Christian, contemporary gospel, praise and worship, hymnody, or hip-hop. What difference do you perceive? Which genre is most comfortable for you?
- How closely does your preaching rhythm parallel the music of the worship service?

Rate and Clarity

In small groups, choose one psalm and take turns following the instructions below and then discussing the questions that follow:

- Read it at your normal rate.
- Read it as slowly as you can.
- Read is as quickly as you can.
- At which rate was the person's speech most intelligible?
- What difficulties did you note in the person's production at each rate?
- Did you detect any difference in pronunciation than what you usually use?
- How many words were mispronounced?
- What rate works best for your preaching, and why?

Rewriting or Substitution of Texts

There are times when the biblical text seems a bit circular and even stilted depending on the translation. Preachers at times stumble over pronunciations or make up words. There are self-pronouncing Bibles as well as Web sites that assist in pronunciation (see above, p. 52).

1. Read over Numbers 1:1-16 or Matthew 1:17, practice the names contained in the text until you approximate the correct pronunciation. Take turns reading the listing and assist each other in pronunciation keeping in mind dialects and regionalisms.

2. Read Romans 1:1-7, rewrite it in a manner in which your congregation or primary preaching location will understand its meaning. Consider the flow of speech, intonation, inflection, and articulation that most closely corresponds to the speech patterns of your primary preaching context. The paraphrase may be helpful in the body of the sermon.

Chapter 5

Embodying the Word

Fredrick is a late-seventy-something, six-foot-three, gray-haired, athletically built, African American Baptist preacher with fifty years of experience. He slowly strides to the podium with his Bible resting in the crook of his right arm. Looking over the top of his glasses, he looks around the chapel as if he is taking everyone in. He leans over the podium as he reads the text, and then confidently begins the sermon without a manuscript. His volume is steady until he approaches a point of emphasis. He pauses, smiles, waves his hand in the air, steps backs, smiles and says, "I think I said something there!" He is not rushed and fleshes out each concept with these movements.

Paula apparently wants to convert her manuscript. She is a thirty-something, full-figure, five-foot-five, white, Presbyterian female. She generally is talkative in class, but today another person has arrived to preach. She approaches the podium with her head down, shuffling her feet. She uses her right hand to move pages but allows her left had to hang limply by her side. She does not look up even after reading her text. Her soft monotone voice is barely audible, yet her content is excellent. She is physically and emotionally disengaged. She almost runs back to her seat when she finishes her twelve-minute sermon.

Chris is in his late forties. He held three pastorates before coming to seminary. He refers to his manuscript rather than reading it verbatim. He laughs easily and speaks with a melodious cadence. His movements and facial expressions match the words of the text as he acts out the content. At several points he throws his head back slightly to the left, smiles, and extends his arms sweeping the room in a welcoming gesture. He relishes the preaching moment and works to ensure that everyone is included in the homiletical exchange.

Embodiment is the act of representing something in a bodily or material form. It occurs when someone speaking uses their physical self to transform an abstract, mental idea into a concrete form, shape, or representation in order to assist in establishing its meaning for the audience. Richard Ward calls for preachers to train their bodies and voices to become responsive to the language, thought, attitudes, and intention of the biblical text. He calls such performance of the text "body thinking."[1] The preachers described above illustrate different levels of ability in using their presence, emotion, and body language to reinforce the meaning of the words used in the sermon.

This chapter will discuss embodiment issues that relate to preaching. These issues include preaching presence, anxiety, and comfort zones in preaching, mood, facial expression, eye contact, posture, amplification, emotion and preaching, text and sermon form, manuscript form, and usage in worship experiences.

Preaching Presence

William Shakespeare's *Hamlet* contains the frequently quoted line, "This above all, to thine own self be true."[2] This piece of advice would serve preachers well. In an age of cloning, pulpit-style plagiarism, everybody is doing it, and one-size-fits-all preaching, there is a need for preachers to reacquaint themselves with their authentic selves. One aspect of authenticity is the preacher's presence. Have you ever met someone who is distinctively different yet has a presence that seems to fill up a room? Have you heard a voice that is so unique that you identify it as soon as the first word flows from the person's mouth, caressing your ears and commanding rather than demanding attention? Perhaps you have watched a person move in the pulpit, seemingly gliding or marching, or being so at ease that you thought they were born in there? These are examples of people comfortable in their own homiletical skin. She has discovered who she is as a preacher and exudes confidence. He understands that he has something to say and does not need to assume another personality to do so. These are examples of preaching presence, the aspects or physicality of a person that command respectful attention. Presence is sometimes viewed as that quality of self-assurance and effectiveness that allows the preacher to achieve rapport with the congregation. Authentic preaching presence is absent caricature or stereotype. The mannerisms, idiosyncrasies, and, at times, eccentricities of the preacher enhance the message and open communication with the congregation.

Authentic preaching is to be conscious of one's unique preaching presence and use it as fully as possible in proclaiming the gospel. One way to do this is to review videos of your own preaching. When reviewing my last few preaching DVDs, I became aware that I do not have a poker face. I reflect my emotions in my eyes and the right corner of my mouth. Frowning, smiling, pouting, pursing, tensing, relaxing lips are conjoined with blinking, squinting, staring, closing, darting, contemplating, and wide eyes—surprised eyes. I also use my hands to elaborate on statements, roll my shoulders when transitioning between points, rock back and forth at particularly emotional points, occasionally strike the podium with my right hand or clap my hands to make a point and may jump up and down or bend over during the celebrative moments. I am a mid-fifties, five-foot-four, full-figured, African American female. My signature look includes shoulder-length salt-and-pepper hair, purple glasses, and three-and-a-half-inch heels that I discard prior to preaching. Due to my height I negotiate where to stand and at times am obscured by the height of the podium. I try to glance at every sector of the sanctuary at some point during the sermon. My emotions run the gamut from abject terror of preaching to overflowing, tear-filled joy of sharing a transformative word. While I resist watching recordings of myself, they assist in discovering my embodied presence. My colleagues and family had described my body language to me, but I did not accept their critique until I began watching myself. Any preacher who is interested in vocally and nonvocally embodying the word of God to the best of one's ability should engage in a discipline of self-analysis of one's preaching presence. There are a number of specific elements of presence that preachers can work on.

Facial expressions are an important external part of embodying and transmitting emotion. The eyes, lips, jaw, forehead, tongue, and nose voluntarily and involuntarily display anger, fear, sadness, disgust, surprise, contempt, embarrassment, and enjoyment. The challenge for the preacher is not only to be aware of her expressions but also to know how the expressions affect the transmission of words in preaching. She should articulate, "The joy of the Lord is my strength," with a smile on her face and an elevated voice in order to allow the congregation to see and or hear joy. Sporadically, I observe preachers who smile throughout the sermon even when talking about God's judgment or destruction. This gives the appearance of insincerity or extreme tension. Use of facial expressions (along with the voice) should match and interpret the content of what is being spoken.

Use of hands can either aid or distract from the way hearers receive the sermon. Hand movements that are directly associated to the words being spoken—such as raised hands when describing height, pointing up or down to signify heaven or hell, small, precise movements to punctuate words, or sweeping movements to indicate inclusion—elaborate the preached word. There also are preachers who look like they are landing planes as the hands wave around totally unassociated with the texts. At times preacher idiosyncratically self-touch by playing with jewelry, moving hair from eyes, straightening ties, pulling up on belts or earrings, smoothing or wiping the tops of head, stroking beards, fiddling with stoles, buttoning and unbuttoning jackets, jingling coins in pockets, beating the air with Bibles, pointing pens, pushing up glasses, lifting manuscripts, pulling down on sides of skirts or pants, steepling hands, or wiping the corners of their mouths. Each may distract the observer during the message delivery.

The pulpit itself plays a role in preaching presence. The podium can be a particularly daunting wooden, Plexiglas, or metal piece of furniture. While there are hydraulic podiums that are adjusted to fit the height of the preacher, most churches have fixed podiums that vary in height, width, lighting, and physical condition. I have a friend who carries a small Tupperware stool to preaching assignments in order to be seen above the podiums evidently built for six-foot-tall preachers. In the same way, tall preachers complain that many podiums are too low and find themselves bending down to see their manuscripts. Leaning over may mean the preacher seeks to be closer to the listeners or is pleading with them to understand what is being said. Some preachers lean or rest on the podium as if tired or informal in the message intent. Preachers who grip the sides of or bracing on the podium may be indicating tension or uncertainty. Pounding the podium may be assessed as demanding attention or demonstrating authority. Each is indicative of an individual the preacher's physicality and emotional presence. Plexiglas pedestals increase a sense of vulnerability because the congregation can see crossed legs, tapping feet, and twitching hands.

Amplification equipment can greatly enhance sermon delivery, particularly for those with soft voices or in enormous sanctuaries. But quality of equipment must be attended to. Blaring monitors, tinny sounds, or feedback interfere with sermon delivery. Quality of amplification is based on the church budget and choice. Decisions must be made between fixed and wireless microphones; quality, number, and placement of monitors; level of amplifier or soundboard used. Congregations will do well to spend as much as they are responsibly able to do to get amplification equipment that will produce quality sound and last for a long time. But issues involving amplification are not limited to the quality of the equipment purchased. They also include how the equipment is used. Speaking in one's normal volume allows the microphone to be set to the tones in one's voice. Microphones, like telephones, amplify the voice so there is no need to shout into them. If at all possible, have a sound technician check your voice and microphone prior to preaching to avoid a "mic check" after the sermon begins. Likewise, avoid having the technician turn up the volume during the course of the sermon because the people are unresponsive and you assume they cannot hear. This may be a delivery misinterpretation. Being loud does not mean being effective or prophetic. Some microphones require not only the use of your voice but also your hand. Microphones can too easily become a prop for some preachers, particularly when they hold them on, below, or next to their mouths. Some wave them around like scepters. Some are tethered to microphones. Beating on microphones damages them. Work simply to hold the microphone in a way that attention is not drawn to it.

Distractions that may well be beyond the preacher's control also influence preaching presence, specifically how the preacher handles the distraction. Babies will cry, people will laugh, birds will decide to attend service, people will walk, microphones will feedback, fire alarms will sound, people will cough, glasses will fog up, and manuscript pages will float to the floor. Preachers respond in a range of ways: from apologizing for the interruption, requesting the distraction be removed, encountering an inability to speak, to continuing as if nothing happened. There are pluses and minuses to any approach. The actions may be perceived as uncaring, rude, being out of touch, or being one who could preach as the Titanic rested on the ocean floor. It is difficult to predict one's response to a diversion until it occurs. The best advice is to be in the moment and do whatever comes naturally to you at the time of the distraction.

Emotion

Emotion in preaching has a direct correlation to message intent. Preachers are human, emotive creatures. My contention is that although one is called to lead or minister with the people one is also called as a passionate, compassionate human being with emotions that need to be expressed in the pulpit. This should not be taken as permission to "bleed all over the congregation," beat up the congregation, expose too much of oneself, engage in self-therapy, or ignore the emotional temperature of the listener. Emotion, passion, anger, and implosion all have a direct effect on the oral interpretation of the text. Preaching reveals the innermost parts of who we are and how we personally stand in relation to what and with whom we are proclaiming. The weight of emotion directly affects the tone, duration, energy, volume, and quality of one's voice and thus the audience's perception of the preacher and reception of the message.

Preachers are human and possess a full range of human emotions. Some avoid even minimal emotional display in the pulpit. Some dissolve into weeping. Some appear constantly angry (leading children to ask, "Why is God mad?"). Others are numb from the fatigue of pastoral ministry. Whatever the emotion displayed (or withheld), carriers of the word frequently should consider their own lives, preaching contexts, and congregational relationships. Learning to identify and manage the emotional interconnectivity of person, message and congregation is indispensable in avoiding an expressive implosion when preaching. Individual, ministerial, and congregational factors all affect how preachers may be true to themselves and their emotional barometers.

Individual factors that may affect one's emotional expressions include personal beliefs and theology, effects of culture (isms), family dynamics and support, health, lifestyle, "personal baggage," age, gender, authority issues, communicative style, problem solving, self-critique, or relationality. Congregational factors that affect the preacher emotionally and may have an impact on speech and language production include demographics and relationships, sermon preparation time, competing ministerial responsibilities, worship or ritual leadership, mismanaged expectations, annual special-day events, community events, and congregational illnesses or deaths. Each area yields a different emotional weight on different preachers and may affect his or her vocal production.

In addition to the individual and ministerial factors that may overshadow or interject emotional qualities into the preaching moment, *performance anxiety* may be present. It has been reported in various trivia books and psychological studies that the number-one fear people possess is the fear of public speaking, surpassing even a fear of death. Seventy-five percent of all people experience some anxiety in public speaking situations.[3] The preacher may fear appearing foolish, rejection by the listeners, comparison to other preachers, uncertain of his abilities, overwhelmed by the awesome nature of preaching, "letting God down," unprepared, or uncertain of her call. Performance anxiety is discernible through posture, physical disturbances, quivering voice, loss of voice, shallow breathing, visible tension, desire to avoid speaking, and dysfluencies. It has been projected that around 40 percent of all public speakers experience performance anxiety. I have viewed student preachers who leave the room several times prior to their assigned preaching slot. Physical disturbances range from vomiting to profuse sweating. One student was rushed to the hospital with chest pains. As much as I preach and for as long as I have preached, I still have gastrointestinal disturbances, loss of appetite, headache, voice disruptions, and intermittent insomnia prior to an engagement. It takes me about a minute into sermon delivery to calm down and find my comfort zone. Web sites advertise and telephone directories propose everything from hypnosis to surgery to alleviate performance anxiety for public speaking. There are simpler ways to alleviate performance anxiety, even if some level of nervousness may always be present. There is an old saying that "practice makes perfect"—the well-prepared and well-rehearsed preacher will have less to be anxious about. Knowledge of the congregation and support systems lessens the fear. Perfectionists may have difficulty with relaxation, but allowing your normal communication skills and natural, nurtured faith to aid in preaching is essential. Preaching is not a competitive sport, although comparison seems to be part of the fabric of many lives. When preachers recognize that different voices, theologies, images, and styles are equally effective in transmitting the gospel, they may begin to appreciate their own unique preaching style, sermon form, and delivery.

Voice, Diction, and Sermon Form

In my classes students are asked to complete a preaching self-assessment at the beginning of the semester. The evaluation information provides a snapshot of the class composition and reminds the preachers of their homiletical underpinnings. The assessment questions include estimated number of sermons preached; frequency of preaching; denominational affiliation; role models; sermon styles; textual translations; average number of texts used in a sermon; preaching passion; hermeneutical process; sermon files and form—manuscript, notes, outline, extemporaneous; expected or average length of sermon preparation and delivery; and the individual's process of self-critique.

The sermon form is a function of the preacher's choice, the form of the focus biblical text and the preacher's style of style of delivery. The exegesis, meditation on the text, and construction of the sermon is a result of the preacher's individuality, cultural tradition, denominational requirements, liturgical season and textual form. Introductory preaching texts, modifications by experienced preachers, and evolving delivery styles provide a cursory list of and description of sermon forms. Several sermon genres may be combined in one sermon.

1. *Topical*—truth or importance of a topic or theme; the preacher allows logical points to control the sequence of the sermon.
2. *Textual*—follows the parts, divisions, pericopes, or sequences of thought in the text
3. *Expository*—addresses an extended passage of Scripture, centering attention on one emphasis in the passage—a teaching, insight, promise, hope, warning, character, experience, meaning, prophecy, virtue, key word
4. *Narrative*—basic story elements of character, plot, setting, and movement

5. *Dialectical*—thesis (what God is doing in text), antithesis (counterpoint of real-life issue), synthesis (juxtaposition of thesis and antithesis)
6. *Polar opposites*—comparative and contrasting points of view, characters, events
7. *Wesley quadrilateral*—consideration of Scripture, tradition, reason, experience
8. *Rhetorical*—convince hearers by application of reasoning, interrogatories
9. *Variations*—dialogue, drama, news reports, musical, multimedia[4]

One should know what works best for the congregation's receipt of information, God's message in the form or complexity of the scriptural text, and the preacher's ability to embody the text in the particular form.

The form of the sermon is of particular import in sermon delivery. The tone and sequences of the narrative may coincide with the preacher's verbal engagement of the text. For example, when preaching about the "man at the temple gate" in Acts 3, one's voice might swell in volume and intensity as the man rises to walk for the first time in his life. The preacher might present different voices for a character sermon or raise and lower the voice to underscore the polar-opposites comparison. Choosing to dramatize a text requires building vocal gymnastics. Vocal variations are critical to prevent textual, expository, dialectical, or quadrilateral sermons from becoming monotone and dull.

On a cautionary note, annually preachers should stretch themselves by adding new forms, styles, illustrations, and delivery embodiment to their preaching presentation portfolio. Those traditionally using only narrative may fall into a monotonous pattern of three stories and a joke. Those only opting for expository forms may lack variety in imagery an illustration. I recommend that students have at least three different forms or combinations of forms in their preaching repertoire to avoid predictability in the pulpit. Likewise, those who always stand behind the podium may move out and use a different form. Those who always run back and forth may exchange running shoes for standing shoes. Remember that running does not mean engaging and standing does not mean boring. The individual's vocal embodiment, physical presence, and sermon content each contribute to explication of God's "priestly listenings."

Manuscript or Extemporaneous Delivery

Preachers and laity alike often debate whether the best preachers use a manuscript or preach extemporaneously. I do not want to argue for one method over the other—different preachers have different styles and strengths—but to comment on how each can aid or hinder sermon delivery. Some preachers carry their words with them into the pulpit in some written form, using a manuscript, notes, or outlines. These written words may be handwritten or printed on a computer; they may be on note cards, yellow legal pads, or plain paper; they may be held in an elaborate leather binder, a simple manila folder, folded into a Bible; or they be on a laptop sitting on the podium, a PDA held in the hand, or something resembling a teleprompter standing near the pulpit. For convenience's sake, we will use "manuscript preacher" to refer to anyone who uses any of these types of methods.

Being a manuscript preacher can be a hindrance to delivery or serve the communication loop well. To be a manuscript preacher is be tethered to the podium. Some manuscript preachers are snugly bound to the pulpit, so much so that their head is bound downward. They read rather than reference their manuscripts, and congregations are left to overhear the sermons instead of being addressed. Other manuscript preachers, however, are more loosely tethered. The cords tying them are still relatively short—they do not walk away from the pulpit—but they do not tie the preacher's head down. These preachers are comfortable at the podium. They stay put but their eyes are focused upward on the hearers instead of downward at the podium. Still other manuscript preachers are tethered by a longer line. They are able to use written material and yet move around in the pulpit. They step away from the pulpit, giving the congregation a sense of intimacy with them. They return to the pulpit regularly to glance down at their manuscript as they make the next sermonic move, but their eyes do not linger down for long. While this can be effective in giving the congregation a sense that the preacher is speaking more extemporaneously, some of those who move around a lot are unable to give organized sermons. Their sermons wander like their feet. They resort to a diatribe or listing of scriptural texts or song titles.

Although the word *extemporaneous* means composed or spoken unexpectedly or on the spur of the moment, *extemporaneous preaching* actually takes careful preparation. Some interpret preaching without notes as meaning the sermon is divinely inspired, closer to God, or filled with God's Spirit. One is thought, in many faith systems, to be a great preacher if he stands before the people sans manuscript. Indeed, people who think this way tend to criticize manuscript preachers as being "trapped behind the pulpit," disengaged, too stiff in posture or less conversational with the congregation than are extemporaneous preachers. The truth of the matter is that many people are able to present extemporaneous sermons but choose not to due to their learning channels such as information processing, the need for visual cues, or the need for assurance that they will not forget something. Some of the "great preach-ers" of the twentieth century wrote full manuscripts and memorized them. The late Dr. Frederick Sampson never took a manuscript into the pulpit but wrote his notes on an envelope kept in the inside breast pocket on his jacket just in case he needed it to jog his memory. Dr. Gardner C. Taylor memorized his full manuscript then wrote three or four words on a piece of paper for prompts.

I am generally a full manuscript writer and reference, rather than read, the manuscript while preaching. I am most comfortable standing behind the pulpit but am active in hand gesture and body movement. At other times I find myself holding a microphone and moving around the pulpit area or into the congregation. I do not know when this will occur but the call and response of the congregation, the type of sermon form, the sermon content, and the unction of the Holy Spirit are all contributing factors. I also preach extempo-raneously when called for by the context, sermon type, and amount of time for preparation and rehearsal allows. It is good, on the one hand, for preach-ers to find the method that best suits them—be it using a full handwritten or typed manuscript, outline, notes, laptop, handheld device, or no notes at all—but it is also good for preachers to learn different methods of preaching. The preacher's level of preaching experience, comfort level, familiarity with the biblical text, attention to detail, organization of thoughts and practice contribute to whether he or she primarily preaches with or without notes. The safest move is to use whatever works best for you, and then experi-ment with other methods from time to time. Just remember that as a written manuscript can be unorganized, disjointed or trite, an extemporaneous ser-mon can be jumbled, disconnected, or boring. Conversely, the same divine inspiration is present whether one preaches with a manuscript, with notes, or from memory.

Preaching and Worship

Liturgist and homiletician Thomas Troeger stipulates that worship is shaped in the memory of the "body" through walking, kneeling, talking, writing, and speaking.[5] Each worship setting has acceptable standards and understood boundaries for oral performance and silence. Worship creates a sense of com-munal inclusion, shared beliefs and values, and allows persons to perceive opportunities for life transformation. Preaching is an offering of the people (of the preacher) to God. Another homiletician who argues for a close rela-tionship between sermon and liturgy is Charles L. Rice. He claims that liturgy gives the preacher opportunity to lead the congregation in the direction of making vital connections with God, one another, and with the preacher. There are preachers whose individuality disappears when they enter the preaching moment. They seamlessly allow the text and content not their personality to speak. Their purpose for preaching is to communicate God's words to God's people. When the preacher is motivated by a disconnected ego or preaching stage presence the result is disembodied preaching.[6] I find myself amazed at the disconnect some preachers have with the fuller liturgical celebration of the congregation due to viewing the sermon as the "star moment," thinking that the entire worship service revolves around their presence or absence. Indeed, some contemporary preachers do not enter the sanctuary until the designated preaching time and then leave the sanctuary as soon as the sermon ends. I advise students to participate in all aspects of worship, prelude to recessional, in preparation for preaching and building the faith community. The worship experience allows the preacher to absorb the attitudes, opinions, emotions and faith of the people, and she may be able to incorporate much of it in delivery and, at times, modified content.

Passion in the pulpit is the underlying theme that characterizes most of our discourse in this chapter. Regardless of where we begin, that passion steps from the corners of the mind into the midst of the conversation. It may be subtle or pronounced, smoldering or blazing, soft or loud, but the passion should be ever-present in the sermon. It is the lens that overlays each text. It determines how we embody the sermon. As the bard would say, whatever you attempt in relating the word, make sure it is authentically you and not the result of pressure to be like someone else. Preaching is worship and not a separate entity. The fully invested preacher understands that all elements of worship working together lead the congregation—and the preacher—into a deeper individual and communal conversation with God.

Exercises for Embodying the Word
Presence and Delivery[7]
Reflect on the following questions:

1. What emotions do you feel before, during, or after the proclaiming moment?
2. Consider your posture and use of space. What does the congregation see?
3. Is your voice generally calm, undulating, muted, loud, "normal," raspy, etc?
4. Consider your facial expressions: How do you transmit emotion?
5. What are your body language, eye contact, and energy level like?

For a regular church context, take note of the following considerations:

1. Seating in pulpit, comfort, height, distance to podium, type of podium, carpet or tile.
2. What do you see? Who or what is in your line of vision?
3. What type of amplification is in the sanctuary?
4. Use of lectionary or self-selection of text?
5. Are you responsible for reading the text prior to preaching?
6. Place of sermon in liturgy, how long the congregation attends to the sermon, usual sermon length, response.
7. Presence of allergens, lights, smells, distractions.
8. Length of service, your responsibilities other than preaching.
9. Use of cameras, video or still, recordings.
10. Time of service.

Do You Like the Way You Move?

Record two or three sermons in varied settings. Watch each one without the sound and answer the following questions:

1. What emotions are being related?
2. What does your face signal?
3. How do your posture, gestures, mobility, or head movement embody the sermon?
4. What works? What does not work?
5. Compare and contrast the nonvocal sermons.
6. Watch the sermons again with sound and answer the same questions. Then ask,
7. What would you modify in your delivery to enhance the communicability?
8. What would you retain?

Embodying the Text Exercises

Read each of the following texts to discern the emotion within the writing: Genesis 1 (or read James Weldon Johnson's "The Creation" as an alternative); Exodus 15:1-20; 1 Samuel 2:1-10; Isaiah 40; Luke 1:46-55; 1 Corinthians 13; Revelation 7:9-17.

Imagine yourself in the text, as the author or a character. How would you read the text to ensure that the listener perceived every emotion you sense? If working alone, record yourself as you practice in a mirror. If working with a partner or small group, have the listener(s) write down emotions expressed. Discuss what you were trying to impart and what was received in terms of:

- Authenticity
- Language
- Facial expression
- Voice
- Nonverbal cues

Homiletical Resources for Using Your Imagination

In the introduction to *Imaging the Sermon,* Tom Troeger repeatedly asks, "Preacher, what do you see?"[8] Henry Mitchell, in *Celebration and Experience in Preaching,* says that the effective preacher makes the Word vivid and alive.[9] The preacher is charged to be open to viewing life scenes; Jesus' teachings were infused with observations of life.[10]

Preaching can become stagnant when the preacher constantly uses the same approach to the text. The following exercise is a group exercise designed to expand the preacher's imagination, challenge the preacher with a different approach to a text, to envision often overlooked homiletical information, and to evoke discussion of what truly effective preachers see. Begin by reading and biblical text from the following list. Imagine you are the object listed and that you are reporting what you see, hear, smell, feel, etc.

Character	Text
Walls of Jericho	Joshua 6:2-20
Tomb	Matthew 27:62-66
Sea	Exodus 14:21-28
Perfume	John 12:1-7
Lost Coin	Luke 15:8-10
Garden at Gethsemane	Mark 14:32-42
Hot Coal	Isaiah 6:1-7
Prison	Acts 16:25-30
Sword	1 Kings 3:16-28

1. Describe yourself.
2. How did you become a part of the story?
3. Describe your surroundings. What do you see?
4. Who are other characters in the story? Who do you see?
5. From your vantage point, what is happening?
6. What do you think about what is happening?

7. How does God work within the situation?
8. Act out the text first without sound, then with sound effects and words.

Emotion and Preaching Exercise

Henry Mitchell says that the preacher provides an opportunity for the congregation to grieve, rejoice, think, and share. The preacher, according to Richard Ward, is a prism. Preachers are called to be passionate, compassionate humans who express emotions in the pulpit as invitation for hearers to experience the sermon emotionally.

1. Consider and select *one* of the following texts: Nehemiah 8:10; Ephesians 4:26; Revelation 7:17; Proverbs 17:22; Matthew 5:12.
2. Compose a three-to-five-minute mini-sermon. You may use notes.
3. Please stay with or work the text selected. Avoid preaching around the text, ignoring the text, or opting to preach another text because you are unfamiliar with one of those listed.
4. Peer critique
   a. Observe the content and overall delivery of the person preaching.
   b. Peers will be given one to two minutes to share constructive criticism with you. At this time the one being critiqued may not answer a question but is to listen.
   c. The person preaching will then have one minute to answer or respond to peers.

Handout on Extemporaneous Preaching[11]

This is an informational summary on extemporaneous preaching. It may also be used for long-range sermon planning. It is by no means exhaustive. Your personal experience, denominational polity, opportunities for preaching, and "role models" determine your eventual method/s of preaching extemporaneously.

1. Preaching without notes takes more rather than less preparation.
2. Every second of your life, each experience prepares you for the next sermon.
3. Spend personal devotional time reading a variety of passages from the Bible.

4. Dialogue with the text; talk with others about their perceptions of the text.
5. Pray.
6. Begin a sermon notes file when ideas come up, or tape-record them.
7. Develop a filing system with topics and texts as you think of them; for example, 1 John 3:11—"Serious Love."
8. Watch television, read varied news media, listen to all types of music, observe not only people but also arts and entertainment.
9. Listen to conversations rather than always talking.
10. Ask persons about their interests, concerns, joys, and sorrows—the human condition.
11. From time to time, write sermon briefs, outlines, or manuscripts of the sermon you always wanted to preach or on your passion. Put the notes in your Bible or carry them in your brain marked "To Preach or not to Preach."
12. Practice sermons aloud, tape yourself, or join a preaching group to provide yourself with practice preaching time.
13. Pray for illumination.
14. Reflect on the times that you have heard the text preached. The Bible says there is nothing new under the sun. Avoid plagiarism but think of any insight you have heard or thought of in terms of the assigned text or topic.
15. If you are to choose the text, use one familiar to you. Choose a text that preaches itself, for example, John 1:1.
16. Think about the season of the liturgical calendar, lectionary, annual day, etc.
17. Reflect on a blessing, testimony, witness, song, poem, story (remember that the text rather than the illustration predominates).
18. Be yourself.
19. Be creative, imaginative.
20. Release the Word within you.
21. Meditate on 2 Timothy 4:2.
22. Know your listeners.
23. Reflect on current themes.
24. Use all of your senses: will and intellect; heart and mind; emotion and cognition; obedience and scholarship; experience and erudition.
25. Trust God to place the words in you mind and mouth.
26. Pray.

Preaching in Worship Exercise

Consider what type of sermon fits a particular type of worship service, congregation, liturgical event.[12] What might a sermon on Romans 10:14-15 sound like in each of the following contexts?

Figure 5.1

Type of Worship	Traditional	Convergent (Blended, Diversified)	Contemporary (Praise and Worship)	Emerging
Possible Sermon Forms	Exegetical, Textual, Topical, Doctrinal, Three Point, Narrative	Narrative, Bipolar, Rhetorical, Topical, Textual	Music and sermon receive equal attention, Plays, Topical, Narrative, Epistolary, Experimental	Dependent on context and preacher, any combination from the other three categories
Proposed Delivery Styles and options	Extemporaneous, Full Manuscript, Outline, Notes, Call and Response	Extemporaneous, Full Manuscript, Outline, Notes, Call and Response	Drama, Musicals, Multimedia, Games, Charismatic Call and Response	Ecumenical, Multinational, Missional, Expressive

Chapter 6

Animating the Word

The medium-built, fiftyish, African American, male chaplain wears his dress whites to class on the day he is assigned to preach. He clutches the Bible with the white pages of his manuscript fluttering as he briskly moves to the front of the room. He knows he is a preacher. He rushes through the respect-filled protocol of the COGIC church, recognizing the listeners. Then, like a boxer who enters the ring and hears the first bell, he launches into the text with measured, perfect articulation. Focusing on Revelation 3:1-6, he rises on his tiptoes as he addresses heaven and pirouettes as he says that it is time for us to "turn around before it is too late." Finally, he approaches two students on the first row who high-five him as he reaches the celebrative ending of the sermon. The room erupts in applause, amens, and hallelujahs. The sermon lasts for twenty minutes, but it seems like only five to the listeners, and they are encouraging Walter to continue preaching.

I call his name, but the assigned preacher has left the room unobserved. I contemplate his abrupt absence just as he enters the door reading John 10:10 in a moderately loud voice. He approaches each window and with imagined effort tries to open them. Rhodes, a white, Baptist minister, rechecks the doors and then moves back to a window, which he opens and sticks his leg out as if he was leaving by that route. Arriving at the podium he pauses, rereads the text, and then launches into a homiletical journey about security against thieves. Dressed in all black, he gives the appearance of being judicial. He acts out different ways people steal and how they are caught as he preaches without a manuscript. As he completes the sermon, he leaves the room reading the text from a paraphrased translation.

This day she looks unusually plain, almost invisible. Kim wears a dull brown, floor-length duster that blends in with her skin tone. Her hair is pulled back in an untidy bun, and her face holds no trace of makeup. When I call her name, she bends over, wraps an equally dull shawl around her head and launches into her character. This black, female, United Methodist minister becomes the woman bent over in Luke 13:10. She preaches the first part of the text bent from the waist down looking toward the floor. She talks about what she sees in the dust. Her animation includes labored breathing, wiping her brow, guttural to muffled voice, shuffling her feet, pausing every few steps, keeping one hand on the small of her back, and leaning on the wall. She remains in that position for about six minutes as she discusses what it means to be spiritually ill. As she approaches verse 13, she slowly stands up and finishes the sermon upright but continues to hold her back as she discusses types of spiritual healing as distinct from physical cures. Following the sermon she remains in character for about five minutes.

The contemporary image of the preacher is of a person dancing or stomping back and forth across the pulpit, arms gyrating as if directing a plane in for landing, sweat profusely cascading down the neck and ending in dark pools under each arm. Men and women may opt for brilliantly colored, clinging knit suits or for swaying, professionally tailored robes billowing like clouds with each step. Eyes accusingly pierce the gathered masses or focus on the camera lens or teleprompter. Emphatic voices raise and fall in ear-deafening crescendos, trickle out of pursed lips like a muddied stream, or slide easy notes to the ears of the waiting congregation. Nonverbal communication has been touched upon in the preceding chapter as integral to language, culture, voice, diction, and embodiment. This chapter will contain more specific information about proxemics (space, distance between preacher and listener), haptics (tactile, interpersonal physical contact with listeners, touch), kinesics (body movement, gestures, self-touching, and posture), chronemics (meaning, structure and use of time, speed of body movement) and physicality (attire, body type, hair, and clothing).[1] These factors occur concurrently with or without verbalization. One may have an exemplary manuscript, be exegetically sound and well organized, but still the ultimate effectiveness of the sermon is affected by these nonverbal elements.

Nonverbal Communication
Nonverbal language has an impact on the level of understanding during the preaching moment. It is present whenever the listener is aware of the speaker. A right-brain hemisphere process, nonverbal communication supplements the verbal communication process. It is important to remember that nonverbal communication is important to those with hearing impairment and is more

than sign language. The expression and reception of sign language is a basis for judgments, prejudice, stereotypes, and barriers to "hearing the preacher" or attending to the spoken word. Hands waving without any connection to the text, frowns while preaching about joy, gripping the podium as if it was the last Krispy Kreme donut in the box, pacing like a ball in a tennis match are just a few of the nonverbal language issues in preaching.

Logosomatic language is the material experience of what we see during the preaching event. It enables us to order our reality (logos) through bodily (somatic) experience. Thomas Troeger writes of logosomatic language as a combination of the Word (Gk., *logos*) and movement. He suggests that the preacher experiences the "full bodily weight of truth" using this homiletical vehicle.[2] I refer to logosomatic language as the embodiment and animation of words. The preacher's vocalics—rhythm, resonance, control, and pauses—should be coordinated with his or her nonverbal language. Nonverbal language expresses emotion. It affects information processing and comprehension. It assists in or impedes the preacher in persuading the listeners. Personality, culture, race, and gender cues are imbedded in nonverbal communication.[3] In an age replete with cyberspace, vivid media, short attention spans, and a maturing population with accompanying health- and age-related deficiencies, the preacher must also use all the senses to undergird the spoken word.

Preaching Space and Contact

Proxemics is the study of cultural, behavioral, or social distance between the preacher and other individuals or groups.[4] The term was coined in the late 1950s by linguist Edward Hall. *Haptics*, the study of interpersonal physical contact with listeners, is intricately associated with proxemics. Appropriate physical distance varies by the age, race ethnicity, gender, and culture of the communicative participants. Different types of messages require different amounts of distance for perception of speech. There are different types of spatial arrangement in the preaching event.

The informal zone is termed one's "personal bubble," which varies with each individual. Intimate distance ranges from body contact to approximately six to eighteen inches. This arrangement entails embracing, touching, or whispering. There may be extensively close contact or noncontact in a close space. In contemporary churches the preacher may ask someone to "Turn to your neighbor and say . . ." Or the preacher may move out into the congregation and lay his or her hand on someone's shoulder. A space that keeps each together at "arm's length" but allows conversation between close friends is about two-and—a-half to four feet and is called personal distance. There are different types of touches like power handshakes, hands on shoulders, hugs, intimate touches, and so on. The repercussions of violating one's personal space is important information for preachers who like to walk around the congregation and constantly touch people. Some preachers report that touching makes them more accessible, "one of the people," and more conversational. However, piercing the personal bubble may lead to withdrawal, anxiety, discomfort, a sense of crowding, verbal aggression, avoidance, and physiological responses from the listener.[5] This is crucial when the preacher is a large or tall person or a different gender and the congregant is smaller, caught off-guard, or introverted. I caution preachers that one never knows who wants to be touched unless we ask if it is all right prior to the sermon. Asking during the sermon may lead to embarrassment for both parties. The preacher should attend to the appropriate social and emotional boundaries of the particular.

Business associates and new acquaintances usually maintain social distance. They share information across a space of four to ten feet. This space is also useful for informal interactions with a physical barrier such as a desk, chair, counter, or lectern separating the conversation partners. Social distance assists in maintenance of culturally conditioned margins. Some preachers feel more comfortable elevated in a pulpit or behind a podium. This does not necessarily signal dislike or fear. Church architecture and denominational standards may require the preacher to maintain a business or professional distance. Guest preachers may fall into the new acquaintance category and may use voice, hand gestures, and body movement to establish a connection with the listeners rather than intimate or personal touching.

Public speaking space is twelve to twenty-five feet. Public space is generally desired among strangers although public transportation and seating in sanctuaries changes the comfort zone. In twenty-first-century coliseum- or stadium-design sanctuaries, the distance between the preacher and the congregation may exceed a hundred yards or more. Balconies also increase the interpersonal distancing of speaker and listeners. Holographic (a process by which three-dimensional images can be stored and reproduced using laser light[6]) preaching at some multicampus megachurches, which allows the pastor to "preach" from a single location, has not been fully researched and will require a new category of preaching proxemics. Speech must be projected or amplified in public spaces. The addition of multimedia screens placed around the sanctuary or in overflow rooms also decrease the public speaking space.

Kinesics

Kinesics is the study of communication through bodily movements, such as eye contact, facial expressions, gestures, self-touching, and posture. The face, as an organ of emotion, is probably the most powerful channel of nonverbal communication. People are able to ascertain whether another person likes or dislikes them, their identity, age, humor, and background by watching a pout, frown, smile, smirk, glare, or even a blank face. The face gives the listener cues about the preacher's emotions like anger, concentration, contempt, desire, disgust, excitement, fear, happiness, puzzlement, sadness, and surprise. Not only do facial expressions reveal something about what the preacher is feeling, they invite emotional response. Facial expressions are contagious. If the preacher is smiling, others will likely smile. If the preacher is frowning, congregants will begin to frown. Moreover, the text comes to life in correlation with the preacher's plasticity of the face that allows them to emote.

In conjunction with facial expressions, *oculesics*, or eye contact and usage, helps establish the preacher's credibility and authenticity. Eye gaze—looking hearers in the eye or aversion—like looking over the listeners rather than at them—may trigger an assessment of one's being trustworthy, lying, or fearful. A preacher who wears glasses has an added dimension to think about in relation to eye contact. One should guard against dramatically taking her glasses off at an empathic point of the sermon, since looking over the top of the glasses may appear judgmental. Chewing on the earpiece points to nervousness. Glasses hanging around the neck are associated with a superior attitude. The preacher who decides not to wear glasses or contacts but requires magnification might want to consider increasing the size of the printing font to avoid squinting or misreading.

Moving south from the head, we turn to the preacher's use of her or his hands. Gestures have different meanings in different contexts and cultures, including some cultures' use of specialized hand movements to accompany verbalizations. Broadly speaking, gestures are classed as exuding confidence (open) or defensiveness (closed) depending on the situation and the person reading the gestures. Consider the examples in figure 6.1 (p. 80).

Because of the performance anxiety and the distance involved in preaching, preachers often use mannerisms that are larger than life. The preacher's body language, approach to the pulpit, the walk between the chair and the podium, the rigidity or looseness of the body, the facial expressions, willingness to "get ugly for Jesus," and use of the space at the podium, speaking loudly about one's confidence level and investment in the text—all these come under this category. Gestures in preaching should be as natural as gestures in one-on-one, face-to-face, normal conversation.

Chronemics

Chronemics is the study of structure and use of time and the speed of body movement. The question of the use of time enters the realm of delivery in the

Figure 6.1 • Open and Closed Gestures

Open Gesture	Closed Gesture
open hands	hand covering mouth, nose, hair twisting
palms up	making fists, pounding, tapping, gripping
rubbing palms together	peering over top of glasses
spontaneous eye contact	glancing at door, floor
smile	frown, poker face
feet slightly apart	hand wringing
relaxed posture, leaning forward	rigid posture, locked ankles
hands away from face	legs crossed, folded arms, shaking foot
calm use of facial movements	lack of eye contact, staring, closed eyes
head tilted to one side	hands on hips
	leaning away
	taut lips
	squinting
	hands locked behind back, in pockets
	constant adjusting of clothing

variation of sermon and worship service length among denominational cultures. First, the sermon. Conflict and critique may arise when preachers from one tradition enter another and discover their twelve-minute sermon is rejected as a "speech." Preachers who claim they need "thirty minutes to warm up" may find themselves at a loss in trying to collapse the content to fill a twenty-minute preaching slot. My students practice preaching an entire sermon in one- to three-minute and three- to five-minute spans with the understanding that it is easier to expand extemporaneously than shrink sermon content.

Second, the duration of the service. Some services are timed to be thirty minutes and no more. The preacher must attend to other aspects of worship when writing out of respect for other participants. I have preached in quite a few services that went on for two hours before I preached. I learned to conserve my energy or anxiety and rest when necessary in order to be ready to preach with or without a full congregation.

Finally, the speed of body movement is determined by physicality, musculature, general health, fatigue, and personality. Some preachers are filled with energy and move rapidly in the pulpit. Others seem almost lethargic in engaging the moment. Given the competing demands of ministry and the fear that some preachers may not exhibit self-care is foundational to speed of body movement. Practicing the sermon and immersing one's self in the text, even becoming the characters or objects, is one way to increase physicality.

Exercises for Animating the Word

Holistic View of Passages/Immersion in the Text Exercise

Purpose: To make the passage come alive for a person who has a diminished sense perception or acuity; a child; a person who believes the Bible or, at least, sermons are boring; or anyone else who is part of the preaching moment.

1. Select one of the listed passages: Genesis 1:1-19 (creation); 1 Kings 17:8-16 (widow at Zarephath); Isaiah 6:1-8 (vision of the Lord in the Temple); Luke 23: 44-49 (crucifixion); Acts 3:1-10 (beggar healed at Temple entrance); Revelation 21:1-8 (second coming of Christ)

2. Describe the elements in terms of the following classifications:
   Sensory data
   - Colors
   - Sizes
   - Shapes
   - Smells
   - Textures
   - Sounds
   - Tastes
   - Movements
   - Temperature (humidity, heat, cold)
   - Distances (use of space within the text)
   - Emotions (love, hate, anger, apathy, jealousy, rage, fear, etc.)
   - Tactile sensations/what or how does the surface of skin feel (dry, moist, cold, hot, clammy, rough, uncomfortable, comfortable, irritated, throbbing, etc.)
   - Body positioning, physically, location of characters in relation to each other

3. What is going through your head as you read the passage?

4. Act out the text using your senses.

Physicality and Proclamation Exercise
The purpose of this exercise is to increase use of the skeletal-muscular system to facilitate communication.

1. Choose, read carefully, and study one of the following biblical texts: Genesis 11:1-9; 2 Kings 5:1-14; Jonah 4:5-8; Matthew 9:20-22; Luke 13:10-13; John 15:1-7.

2. In front of a mirror, in a small group, or with a preaching partner act out the text then assess the effectiveness of the presentation in terms of:

- fluidity of movement (Is the person "comfortable" or purposeful in action?)
- adherence to possibilities in the text, that is verbs
- other possible movements associated with the text
- facial expression connected to emotion in text, associated with body movement

3. After the evaluation verbally relate or write your understanding of the text and what information you gained from the movement.

Personal Presentation of the Preacher

This area includes the study of attire, body type, hair, and clothing. In terms of preaching, choice of attire is determined by liturgical occasion, denominational preference, body type and mobility, gender, and self-selection. Clothing evokes meaning and feeling in the speaker and the listener. Some preachers wear regular clothing and others wear vestments. The preacher's choice of whether to robe and, if so, what kind of vestment to wear is dependent on denominational expectations or requirements, the cultural context, and personal preference (these broad categories include theology, type of ministry, geography, church event, and physical comfort or movement). A red robe might be liturgically appropriate in one church and loudly inappropriate in another. Vestments define a clerical office—different robes, stoles, colors, and attendant regalia are often used by different orders of ministry—and set proclaimers apart from the laity. They provide a "covering" from being in the secular to operate as representatives in the sacred, standing as marks of authority and validation of the call to ministry. Pulpit robes come in many forms—handmade to tailored, Afrocentric, traditional ethnic, Wesleyan to cassock, fitted to flowing, costing one hundred or one thousand dollars.

Clergy in some contemporary congregations choose not to invest in ministerial robes, but instead may wear a range of clothes: tailored suits with or without jackets or vests, T-shirts and jeans, caftans, long black skirts and jackets, pantsuits, multicolor shirts with or without collars, large rings and crosses, or muscle shirts plus robe overlays. Many female preachers choose to wear collars and robes as an indicator of ministerial authority. Other women resort to lapcloths as an indispensable part of clergy dress. These eighteen-by-eighteen-inch, usually lace-trimmed, color-coordinated cloths are sold in Christian bookstores, homemade, or sold in specialty boutiques. The point is to cover the preacher's knees if her skirt is short and to be accepted as "ladylike" while she is sitting in the pulpit area.

Preachers who have gray hair, are clean-shaven, or exhibit similar characteristics may be afforded acceptance and respect for "time in service" and "looking like a minister." The congregation identifies with the preacher and trusts that their physical similarities mean similar views. Conversely, preachers with visible tattoos, facial hair, rainbow-colored hair, or innovative robes, or unconventional appearance may have to work on rapport with the congregation and may be sanctioned because of his or her difference.

Attire in Proclamation Exercise

- What is your attire while proclaiming God's Word—robes, suits, dresses, pants, other?
- Is your attire based on tradition, personal preference, senior pastor dictates, other?
- Is there attire that you think is inappropriate for the proclamation moment? Why?
- Are there particular colors that are inappropriate in the pulpit? Why?
- Do you alter your hairstyle in any manner when preaching? Why or why not?
- Is jewelry appropriate? If so, what style, amount, placement?
- Head coverings, lap cloths, shoes, body art?

The preacher's body type, whether large and imposing or small and nondescript, may give mixed signals for both the preacher and the congregation. There may be an assumption that tall, robust people will preach with a certain animation, forthrightness, and "power" that is accepted as "the messenger and message for God." Those whose bodies are smaller may lose some preconceived power points as being "nice" or as presenting a public speech like someone's child or grandchild. Improper maintenance of weight may impinge on voice production and ability to move around the pulpit. More research is needed on the specific cultural responses to preachers with visible disabilities or pregnant preachers. In my experience the responses differ based on the experience of the members of the congregations with disabilities and their stance on women in ministry. In some instances pregnant preachers are asked to remain out of the pulpit until the child is born. In other instances the woman is fully supported as manifesting new life, a biblical principle.

The individual presentation of the preacher may be either a support or barrier to the preaching moment. The reception of the preacher by the listeners is inexorably linked to the person's authentic presence.

⊛ More Exercises for Animating the Word
Person of the Preacher[7]

When evaluating sermons in preaching classes, the emphasis is often exegesis, theology, and overall content. Review a sermon you hear and see using the following categories for a different perspective on the preaching event:

- *Authenticity*—original work, cliché, rote memory, regurgitation, plagiarism, citations, credit
- *Presence*—fearful, energetic, commanding, engaging, tyrannical, domineering, self-righteous
- *Believability*—invested in sermon, committed to content
- *Preaching with listener*—pastoral, prophetic
- *Appearance*—dress, carriage, hair, shoes, colors, vestments, jewelry
- *Communicability*—assessment of levels of language in the listener and preacher, sermon form and transmission of content
- *Audibility*—too loud or too soft, appropriate, good use of varied volume
- *Articulation*—clarity, cluttering, stuttering, pronunciation
- *Dialect*—regional, ethnic, national, cultural
- *Breathing*—breath control, panting, gasping, labored, etc.
- *Pacing and Pauses*—too fast, too slow, variable, too long, pregnant
- *Language usage*—gender, culture, race, geography, denomination, age
- *Nonverbal Communication*—body engagement, language, eye contact, gestures, use of hands, spatial relationships
- *Emotive*—inviting, affirming, demeaning, open to feedback
- *Distractions*—handling, ignored, impact, integration

Conclusion

Jerry has been preaching for forty-one years. He is an average-sized man, five-foot-seven, with curly gray hair and black glasses. He immerses himself in the biblical text but always has an eye and ear on the contemporary world. He is African American, intentionally preaches in a call-and-response mode with content directed at the issues and gifts of the black culture. He is bibliocentric, often expository or topical. He uses a manuscript but references it rather than reads it verbatim. He involves the listeners in the sermon through a series of questions peppered throughout the sermon and during transition to new points. His sermon length is generally thirty minutes. At the same time he preaches in multiple language levels and rarely demeans other denominations or cultures. He uses a handheld microphone and rarely walks around the pulpit area. He uses his voice, facial expressions, and left-handed gestures to embody the sermon. He does not wear a robe but opts for colorful Afrocentric attire. The sanctuary at his church seats about four thousand people and cameras project his image and soft to moderately loud voice to the balcony and those who are seated in the back rows.

Pam, a European American forty-something, is in constant motion. She is about five-foot-five, petite, with a soft voice. She compensates for vocal projection with a headset microphone. She wears a Wesleyan robe, a collar, no jewelry, and her hair pulled back in a ponytail. She skirts the biblical text but tells a series of stories from the life of the congregation. She does not use a manuscript but places note cards on a Plexiglas stand in the front of the sanctuary. She self-describes her preaching as dramatic conversation. She attended the church as a child and has returned after a fifteen-year absence. The congregation smiles and nods their heads as she speaks. Given the median age of her ninety-five-member retiree congregation her animation supplements her speech.

Fred, a preacher's son, is in his late thirties. He is pastor of two church campuses. He preaches in a measured, plain, folksy style replete with props, multimedia, and dramatic interpretation of the biblical text. He utilizes expository and narrative styles primarily. He is casually dressed. His voice is a raspy first tenor, similar at times to Barney Fife of the old Andy Griffith Show. He is at the main campus three Sundays out of the month and simultaneously projects his sermon to one other campus via hologram. The congregation at the hologram service responds in a similar fashion to what is done during the "live" sermon.

In the course of my life, I have listened to countless sermon styles and delivery methods in seminary classrooms, local churches, ecumenical conferences, and through varied media nationally and internationally. At the end of the day, the delivery of the sermon is personal. The receipt of the sermon is personal. Even after all the technical training and rehearsal in front of a mirror, the word of God is transmitted most effectively when we use our natural inclinations of one-on-one speech—regardless of the size of the congregation. Just as each call to preach is distinctive, the voice of each preacher is distinctive. The physical movement of each preacher is different. The way each preacher pronounces a word or reverences God is something no one else can claim.

Many years ago the distinguished homiletician, Gardner C. Taylor, told me that the preacher should approach the work of God like a gourmet meal. It should be served with the palate of the listener in mind. I know my own palate and the tastes of the listeners with whom I regularly preach. I know that presentation is everything. Serving a meal on cracked, dirty, and mismatched plates seems to affect its taste regardless of how well we prepared the meal. If we present a colorful, well-seasoned, thoughtfully prepared meal on clean plates the digestion is generally easier. Some might be tempted to even say the same food tastes differently because the presentation is better.

In our desire to share the word of God, we must prepare to deliver the sermon so that it is palatable for others. The task is to deliver the sermon so that others can gain some spiritual weight. When we are honest with ourselves about our delivery, we will acknowledge that sometimes we put too much seasoning in the meal, over-pronouncing words as if we were auditioning for a Broadway play. Sometimes we undercook the meal, barely twitching a muscle and mutely uttering our words with dispassion, disinterest, and detachment from our listeners. Sometimes, when we attend to the consumers of the word, we adjust or delivery with just the right amount of varied volume, pronunciation, inflection, and body language. The listener, in turn, is then able to respond to the presentation of the meal, allowed to taste the words, often filtering it to suit their tastes, and connecting with the truth in the words regardless of who is presenting it.

Some of us are executive chefs. Some of us are family cooks. Some of us follow the directions of the cookbook verbatim. Some of us cook from memory. Somehow, people are fed. The point of this text has been to assist in enhancing the delivery and reception of the preached word so that no one is left out of the preaching moment or goes away hungry. This is the purpose of delivering the sermon.

Notes

Introduction

1. Cicero, *De Oratore*, I, 31. See also Craig A. Loscalzo, "Rhetoric," in *Concise Encyclopedia of Preaching*, ed. William H. Willimon and Richard Lischer (Louisville: Westminster John Knox, 1995), 409–16, for a historical review of rhetoric.

2. Jon Eisenson, *Voice and Diction: A Program for Improvement*, 7th ed. (Boston: Allyn and Bacon, 1997), 4–26.

Chapter 1 • Communicating the Word

1. Walter Ong, *The Presence of the Word* (New Haven: Yale University Press, 1967), 167–68. See also Walter Ong, *Orality and Literacy* (New York: Melthun, 1983), 2–3 for a fuller discussion of orality.

2. Ludwig Wittgenstein, *Philosophical Investigation* (New York: MacMillian, 1969), 7.

3. Richard Johannesen, "The Emerging Concept of Communication as Dialogue," *The Quarterly Journal of Speech* 62:373–82. See also classic discussions of communication by Reuel L. Howe, "The Miracle of Dialogue," in *The Human Dialogue*, ed. Floyd W. Matson and Ashely Montagu (New York: The Free Press, 1967), and Martin Buber, *I and Thou*, trans. R. G. Smith, (New York: Scribner's, 1958).

4. Lucy Rose. *Sharing the Word: Preaching in the Roundtable Church* (Louisville: Westminster John Knox. 1997), 76–78.

5. Paul van Buren, *The Edges of Language* (London: SCM, 1972), 368–95.

6. *Cambridge Encyclopedia of the English Language*, ed. David Crystal (New York: Cambridge University Press, 1995), 371.

7. Walter Ong, *Orality and Literacy: The Technologizing of the Word,* 2d ed. (New York: Routledge, 2002), 465–78.

8. Henry H. Mitchell, *Celebration and Experience in Preaching* (Nashville: Abingdon, 1990), 79–84.

9. Fred Craddock, *As One With Authority* (Nashville: Abingdon, 1971), 78.

10. Mark Gallie and Craig Brian Larson, *Preaching That Connects: Using the Techniques of Journalists to Add Impact to Your Sermons* (Grand Rapids: Zondervan, 1994), 16–21.

11. Joseph Webb, *Preaching and the Challenge of Pluralism* (St. Louis: Chalice, 2001), 17–30.

12. The language of the sermon is, for me, the most vital part of preaching. However, space does not permit me to explore here issues such as figures of speech (i.e., metaphors, verbal images, analogies, and paradigms), verbal problematics (e.g., clichés, idioms, and jargon), derogatory, exclusionary, or oppressive languages or images, and particularly inclusive

God language, all of which contribute to communicative efficacy or disruption. Some of these topics will be taken up in Jennifer L. Lord's forthcoming contribution to the Elements of Preaching series, *Finding Language and Imagery: Words for Holy Speech*. See also the Elements of Preaching Web site (www.elementsofpreaching.com) for some helpful exercises on language matters.

13. Robert deBeaugrande and Wolfgang Dressler, *The Introduction of Text Linguistics* (London: Longham, 1981), 3–10. This is an adaptation of the authors' paradigm on textual communication.

14. Charles G. Adams, lecture in "Preaching in Black and White," summer school class at Iliff School of Theology, Denver, Colorado, 1987.

Chapter 2 • Inculturating the Word

1. See also Nancy T. Ammerman, Jackson W. Carroll, Carl S. Dudley, and William McKinney, *Studying Congregations, A New Handbook* (Nashville: Abingdon, 1998), chap. 3.

2. Clifford Geertz, *The Interpretation of Culture* (New York: Basic, 1973), 4–13.

3. Dell Hymes, "The Ethnography of Speaking," in T. Gladwin and W. C. Sturtevant, eds., *Anthropology and Human Behaviour* (Washington, D.C.: Anthropology Society of Washington, 1962), 312.

4. See also Charles Long. *Significations: Signs, Symbols, and Images in the Interpretation of Religion* (Philadelphia: Fortress Press, 1986); James Nieman and Thomas Rogers, *Preaching to Every Pew: Cross-Cultural Strategies* (Minneapolis: Fortress Press, 2001); and Joseph Jeter and Ronald Allen, *One Gospel, Many Ears: Preaching for Different Listeners in the Congregation* (St. Louis: Chalice, 2002), for suggestions for preaching in multicultural settings with age, gender, culture, and denominational diversity.

5. Fred Craddock, *As One Without Authority,* 4th ed. (St. Louis: Chalice, 2001), 46–50.

6. Teresa Fry Brown, *Weary Throats and New Songs: Black Women Proclaiming God's Word* (Nashville: Abingdon, 2003), 157–70.

7. Evans Crawford, *The Hum: Call and Response in African-American Preaching,* (Valley Forge: Judson, 1995), 52–64.

8. Jon Michael Spencer, "Folk Preaching (African American)," in William Willimon and Richard Lischer, *The Concise Dictionary of Preaching* (Louisville: Westminster John Knox, 1995), 142–43.

9. Charles E. Debose, "Codeswitching: Black English and Standard English in the African American Linguistic Repertoire," *Journal of Multilingual and Multicultural Development* 13 (1992): 157–67.

10. Carol Myers-Scotton and Walter Ury, "Bilingual Strategies: The Social Function of Code Switching," *Linguistics* 193 (1977): 5–20.

11. Erling Jorstad, *Popular Religion in America: The Evangelical Voice* (Westport, Conn.: Greenwood, 1993), 113–15. See also Jeffrey K. Hadden and Anson Shupe, *Televangelism:*

Power and Politics on God's Frontier (New York: Henry Holt, 1988); and Quentin J. Schultze, *Habits of the High-Tech Heart: Living Virtuously in the Information Age* (Grand Rapids: Baker, 2002).

Chapter 3 • Voicing the Word

1. Jon Eisenson, *Voice and Diction: A Program for Improvement*, 7th ed. (Boston: Allyn and Bacon, 1997), 4–26.

2. Ibid, 17–21.

3. Vocal mechanism image, http://en.wikipedia.org/wiki/Image:Illu01_head_neck.jpg.

4. Ibid. See also G. Robert Jacks, *Getting the Word Across: Speech Communication for Pastors and Lay Leaders* (Grand Rapids: Eerdmans, 1995) for a more "user-friendly" explanation of sound production.

5. Eisenson, *Voice and Diction*, 4, 5.

6. Ibid., 4–26.

7. http://www.asha.org/public/speech/disorders/nodulespolyps.htm, accessed June 27, 2008.

8. American Speech-Language and Hearing Association (ASHA), http://www.asha.org, 2007.

9. Teresa Fry Brown, *Weary Throats and New Songs: Black Women Proclaiming God's Word* (Nashville: Abingdon, 2003), 162.

10. Ibid., 161.

11. Ibid.

12. Ibid., 110–22.

13. ASHA, http://www.asha.org, accessed June 10, 2008.

14. The Stuttering Foundation, http://www.stutteringhelp.org/, accessed June 10, 2008.

15. William Turner, "The Musicality of Black Preaching: A Phenomenology," *Journal of Black Sacred Music* 2, no. 1 (Spring 1988).

16. Evans Crawford, *The Hum: Call and Response in African-American Preaching*, (Valley Forge: Judson, 1995), 15–21.

17. Craig Loscalso, *Preaching Sermons That Connect: Effective Communication Through Identification* (Downers Grove, Ill.: InterVarsity, 1993), 23–29.

18. Ear anatomy image, http://commons.wikimedia.org/wiki/Image:Ear-anatomy-text-small.png. Image released under the GNU Free Documentation License.

19. Lyman Steil, "Toward Better Listening," in Robert Cathcart and Larry Samavor, eds., *Small Group Communication: A Reader* (Dubuque: William C. Brown, 1984), 304–05, originally published in Lyman K. Steil and Larry Barker, *Effective Listening: Developing Your Ear-Q* (Scottsdale: Gorsuch Scarisbrick, 1982).

20. Charles Kelly, "Emphatic Listening," in Cathcart and Samovar, *Small Group Communication*, 296–97.

21. Teresa Fry Brown, Women and Preaching Class exercise, 1997.

Chapter 4 • Articulating the Word

1. See "Direct Map of American English," http://www.geocities.com/yvain.geo/dialects. html or "Linguistic Geography of the Mainland United States," http://www.evolpub.com/ Americandialects/AmDialMap.html, both accessed June 3, 2008.

2. See http://www.pbs.org/speak/seatosea/americanvarieties/ or http://www.american-dialect.org/, both accessed June 3, 2008.

Chapter 5 • Embodying the Word

1. Richard Ward, *Speaking of the Holy: The Art of Communication In Preaching* (St. Louis: Chalice, 2001), 38–39. See also Jana Childers, *Performing the Word: Preaching as Theater* (Nashville: Abingdon, 1998), for performance theory.

2. William Shakespeare, *The Tragedy of Hamlet Prince of Denmark*, vol. 44, part 2, The Harvard Classics (New York: P. F. Collier & Son, 1909–14), Act I, Scene III, ll. 78–80. Polonius prepares his son Laertes for travel abroad with a speech.

3. See David Wallechinsky and Amy Wallace, *The New Book of Lists: The Original Compendium of Curious Information* (New York: Canongate, 2005) and http://www.speech-topics-help.com/fear-of-public-speaking-statistics.html, accessed June 3, 2008.

4. See O. Wesley Allen Jr., *Determining the Form: Structures for Preaching*, Elements of Preaching (Minneapolis: Fortress Press, forthcoming, 2009); Ronald Allen, *Preaching: An Essential Guide* (Nashville: Abingdon, 2002); and Henry Mitchell, *Celebration and Experience in Preaching* (Nashville: Abingdon, 1990), for a more extensive discussion of sermon form. See also Jana Childers, *Birthing a Sermon: Women Preachers on the Creative Process* (St. Louis: Chalice, 2001), for a review of how experienced preachers select sermon form and deliver sermons.

5. Thomas H. Troeger, *Preaching and Worship,* Preaching and Its Partners (St. Louis: Chalice, 2003).

6. Charles L. Rice, *The Embodied Word: Preaching as Art and Liturgy,* Fortress Resources for Preaching (Minneapolis: Fortress Press, 1991), 21, 31, 42–43. See also Brian Blount and Leonora Tubbs Tisdale, eds., *Making Room at the Table: An Invitation to Multicultural Worship* (Louisville: Westminster John Knox, 2001); and David M. Greenhaw and Ronald Allen, *Preaching in the Context of Worship* (St Louis: Chalice, 2000).

7. Teresa Fry Brown, Introduction to Preaching Class exercise, 1997, 2007.

8. Thomas Troeger, *Imaging a Sermon* (Nashville: Abingdon, 1990), 17–18.

9. Henry Mitchell, *Celebration and Experience in Preaching* (Nashville: Abingdon, 1990), 95.

10. Ibid., 26, 56.

11. Teresa Fry Brown, 1997. I have used use this handout for about ten years with students who want to practice preaching without notes. See also Joseph M. Webb, *Preaching Without Notes* (Nashville: Abingdon, 2001).

12. Teresa Fry Brown, excerpts from "Preaching Is Worship Seminar" handout, October 2005.

Chapter 6 • Animating the Word

1. Peter A. Anderson, " Nonverbal Communication in the Small Group," in Robert Cathcart and Larry Samavor, eds., *Small Group Communication: A Reader* (Dubuque: Wm. C. Brown, 1984), 258–70. See also my chapter on attire and delivery in *Weary Throats and New Songs: Black Women Proclaiming God's Word* (Nashville: Abingdon, 2003).

2. Thomas Troeger, *Imagining A Sermon* (Nashville: Abingdon, 1990), 53–56.

3. Judee Burgoon, David Buller, and W. Gil Woodall, *Nonverbal Communication: The Unspoken* Dialogue (New York: Harper & Row, 1989), 4–9.

4. Edward T. Hall, *The Silent Language* (Garden City, N.Y.: Doubleday, 1959), 129.

5. Burgoon, et al., *Nonverbal Communication*, 76–80.

6. http://web.mit.edu/museum/lightforest/holograms.html, accessed June 4, 2008.

7. Teresa L. Fry Brown, Introduction to Preaching handout, 1995–2008.